W9-BDY-479

Insightful Parenting

MAKING MOMENTS COUNT

Insightful Parenting

MAKING MOMENTS COUNT

Dr. Steve Kahn

Family Therapy Press

SAINT PAUL, MINNESOTA

Copyright © 2007 by Steve Kahn

All rights reserved. No part of this publication may be reproduced in any manner whatsoever without the prior written permission of the publisher.

Published by
Family Therapy Press
September 2007
2697 East County Road E
St. Paul, MN 55110

Printed in the United States of America on acid-free paper

ISBN 978-0-9797255-0-0

LCCN 2007904231

Cover and interior text illustrations by Lindsey Kahn
To see other work by the illustrator please go to www.kaianart.com

Cover design by Kyle G. Hunter
Interior text design by Wendy Holdman

To read other articles about parenting by the author or to order additional copies of this book please go to www.drstevekahn.com

Acknowledgments

I want to thank the children and parents who shared their experiences of childhood and family life. Also, thank you to the teachers, counselors, and principals who collaborated with me during the course of my career, and encouraged parents to look at their parenting when their children were having problems.

The ideas that constitute the core message of this book would not have been possible without the models of excellent parenting provided by my wife, Jackie Metelak, and my mother, Edith Fien. Both demonstrate what it means to parent insightfully and bring meaning to the moments of childhood.

The writing of this book benefited from the generous and careful editing by the following friends and colleagues. Since they saw the earliest versions of this book, they know the importance of their contributions! Thank you to Amanda Anderson, Sara Belleau, Ann Blair, Brian Boyd, Scott Bradley, Julie Corty, Libby Dodelson, Edith Fien, Amy Goldwasser, Janet Grochowski, Richard Grochowski, Sarah Ingebrand, Elizabeth Kahn, Gary Kahn, Esther Kallman, Judy LaPanta, Nicole Leff, Colleen Natterstad, Cyndi Neus-Bradley, Mary Oppegaard, Shari Parsons, Donna Patkin, Victoria Safford, Lee Soderlind and Bob Tift.

Special thanks and a huge sense of gratitude to Jonathan Coopersmith, Paul Gasner, Caren Hansen, Jay McNamara, Jackie Metelak, and Michelle Mucha for the line-by-line editing of earlier drafts.

Contents

Chapter 1

Parenting with an Eye on the Future

This book describes how to use the everyday events with our children (the "moments" from the title) to strengthen them, teach them all we can and keep them emotionally close to us throughout their adolescent years. It builds on two important observations from my twenty-five years working with families:

> ➤ Children can begin to have trouble when they become adolescents even if they seemed fine for their first ten or twelve years.
> ➤ *Parenting for adolescence* begins years *before* adolescence.

Children who handle the transition to adolescence successfully seem to have parents who are able to keep an eye on adolescence while dealing with the day-to-day challenges of childhood. One parent described her technique of imagining a split-screen television in front of her—one screen with the present situation and the other set to the future. The "future" screen is always a bit blurry. We can never really know what our kids will be like as teenagers, but the process of keeping an eye on the future highlights that we are setting the stage for adolescence while we are taking care of the day-to-day challenges.

Parents sometimes seek help at the onset of adolescence, thinking that therapy for their children would solve their problems. However, the focus of therapy would often shift from the children to the parents themselves: focusing on perceptions, thought processes, parenting styles and strategies. By then, there may have been years of battles, overreactions and punishments that led to resentments. Other times parents had been too timid and inconsistent with their discipline. *Often parents wish they had come for advice years before.*

From preschool to high school, we deal with moments that provide us with chances to teach our children what they need to learn. Unfortunately, those moments do not come with a sign pointing out: "Here is a teaching opportunity." In fact, the moments can be camouflaged as temper tantrums, sibling rivalry, friendship problems, rude manners, etc. This book will teach you how to find the best teaching opportunities and how to turn a potentially stressful moment with your children into a valuable lesson.

When we can see the teaching opportunities of everyday family life, we are able to find our voice, develop a plan of action and follow through. The term "blind spots" is used to describe the barriers or obstacles that keep us from seeing the teaching opportunities. If we are not able to see them, we may experience problems in the parent-child connection.

GRADUAL EROSION OF INTIMACY

When our children are young, it is difficult to see what adolescence will bring. The relationship between parent and young child that seems so perfect and secure will become "voluntary" as our children move into their teenage years. How we are when they are younger determines if they stay connected with us when they are older. We have to prevent the gradual erosion of intimacy *while we are dealing* with bad manners, incomplete assignments or "forgotten" chores. Parents of teenagers often look back and wish they had not made such pests of themselves over small matters. They are saddened by their lack of perspective for what seemed like major problems. Many say they overreacted to small challenges and did not realize they were wearing out their welcome (in their child's eyes) until adolescence was already in full swing. They "made mountains out of molehills" and their children became "allergic to the sound of their voice." *Tension between parent and child about the problem of the day can set the stage for more serious problems over the years, more than the original problem was worth.*

Two important questions to consider:

> ❯ When you are taking care of today, are you presenting yourself in a way that is likely to lead to more or less intimacy over the years?
> ❯ Will they remember being criticized for every mistake? Or will they remember feeling close to you even at the time of their mistake?

PARENTING WITH A LONG-TERM VIEW

Parenting would be different if it were just for the short-term. The strategies to fix the short-term problems are not necessarily the strategies to produce a healthy adolescent. We have to teach about resilience, emotional calibration, interpersonal skills, and the work ethic, all the while keeping them closely connected to us. Many parents attend to the short-term only. They get out of the door in the morning. Their children do their chores and their homework. They get everyone to their activities and their appointments on time. But, they do all that in a way that leaves them unable to focus on their children's greater needs.

Our children need to learn from us how to be able to take care of themselves emotionally, grow from their mistakes, and bounce back from disappointments. When we keep our eye on these goals, we handle the short-term challenges differently.

One quick boating story. A father told me that parenting reminded him of being on the lake as the sun was setting. If there was a light on shore he could keep his eye on, he would be fine after dark. As long as he could see where he was heading, he would be able to handle being out on the lake after sunset. Without something out there he could see and aim for, he would get lost. This image helped him get through some challenging moments with his children.

Like the light on shore, the five long-term goals listed in Table One and described in the pages that follow, help us stay on track. They highlight the prominent differences between thriving and struggling teenagers. In fact, part of the assessment process at the beginning of therapy includes exploring these five areas. Imagine a therapy session where parents express one of the following concerns they have about their teenager:

> ▸ Low self-esteem, clingy, dependent, unsure of themselves, hesitant to try new things.
> ▸ Underachieving, poor effort/attitude, no "value" of education.
> ▸ Gloomy, negative, isolates, withdraws from family, pessimistic.
> ▸ Lies, withholds information, manipulates, blames others, does not take responsibility.
> ▸ Burst into adolescence, rude, obnoxious, backtalk, temper outbursts.
> ▸ Wrong crowd, risk-taking, adventure-seeking, sexually active, lack of caution, irrational sense of invulnerability.
> ▸ Sense of entitlement, too powerful, cocky, arrogant, boastful, uncompromising, wants to drive their own life but they are not steering.
> ▸ Obsessive worrying, reviews, rehashes and rehearses.
> ▸ Perfectionism, eating disorders, depression.

How we act as we get them moving in the mornings, and see that chores and homework get done, will have implications for how our children handle their responsibilities and their emotions when they are older. For example, if we hesitate to discipline, they might become irresponsible, but if we are too critical they might drift from us.

> ▸ How does a perfectly delightful 6- or 7-year-old become a teenager with low self-esteem?

> What might have happened to the child who later became an underachieving teenager?
> Why would one 15-year-old be gloomy and reclusive day in and day out, while another one might be pleasant most of the time, with just an occasional irritable day?
> Are there parenting strategies that can be followed before adolescence that can decrease the power of peer pressure during adolescence?
> Do parents make it more likely that their children will develop a problem with obsessive thinking or perfectionism by how they handle everyday moments of family life?

Six- and 8-year-old children keep their parents at the center of their universe and tell them everything. There are hugs at morning time and kisses at bedtime. It is hard to imagine that this idyllic chapter of parenting is temporary. We prefer to believe that it will always be this way.

These parents might see 14-year-olds in the neighborhood or at the mall and assume their child will never act that way! Those 14-year-olds must have parents who are not as talented or as loving as they are. *The shift from intimately connected 8-year-old to aloof, maybe even rude, 14-year-old happens very gradually.* But we have to parent every day with adolescence in mind.

One parent described a worthwhile experience she had at a workshop offered to her through her job. The facilitator was warming up the audience and asked people to summarize their parents' legacy in one minute and share that in small group. She said it was not so much her answer about her parents' legacy that was helpful, it was the thought that her children might someday be asked the same question.

How do we hope to be remembered? How would we like our children to answer that facilitator's question? Is there a way to show up, be true to our values, teach our children what they need to learn, and keep them intimately connected to us at the same time? The approach presented here is aimed at helping parents answer "yes" to these questions.

NON-RENEWABLE RESOURCE

It helps to think about parenting as a non-renewable resource, like coal or oil rather than sun or wind. Each moment in parenting only comes around once, and we either make it count or we do not. And we do not have until the day they leave for college! In fact, many parents are surprised to feel their influence decreasing as early as fifth grade, years before the official onset of adolescence.

Similar to other non-renewable resources, we have to conserve parenting resources. One way is to pick our battles wisely. There is a difference between battles that are essential (e.g., health and safety), and those that are not essential (e.g., chores and mealtime behavior). In fact, battles that seem urgent may resolve themselves just with the passage of time. When parents think they need to "nip it in the bud," or "deal with something before it gets worse," their reaction may be more hurtful than helpful.

For example, let us consider a bedroom that is not up to our standards. We have a choice in how to view this event. We could connect a clean room with a privilege (e.g., allowance) or a consequence (e.g., limits on television or the computer) and calmly and confidently wait. We can say to ourselves: "Sooner or later they will figure this out. Even a rat in a maze learns to push a lever to get a food pellet, and my child is certainly smarter than a rat!" This approach does not use up any parenting resources and *will* get the room clean. Not only do we have to take care of the short-term issues (room clean, grades good, nice to siblings, well-mannered), but we also have to help them develop a work ethic, learn to take care of themselves emotionally and interpersonally, become resilient and stay connected to us all at the same time. If we had less to teach (and unlimited resources) there would be less reason to worry about time running out. The long-term goals almost always require a different approach.

We begin to explore this further by studying the long-term goals.

TABLE ONE—LONG-TERM GOALS

1. Resilience

- > What worth is based on
- > Self-esteem is not contingent on a smooth road
- > Anticipate disappointments

2. Emotional calibration

- > Language of feelings
- > Closure
- > Optimism
- > Thoughts precede feelings
- > Change and loss
- > Sizing

3. Interpersonal skills

- > Boundaries and self-advocacy
- > Communication and conflict-resolution skills
- > Compassion
- > Trust
- > Personal growth process
- > Internal locus of control
- > Stress management

4. Connected to us

- > Perceive us accurately as their reservoir of confidence
- > Logical consequences by loving and forgiving parents

5. Work ethic

- > Defer gratification and develop patience
- > Cooperate with authority
- > Importance of education
- > Ability to work with anyone

1. RESILIENCE

The three skills that help children become resilient are as follows: 1) understanding what worth is based on, 2) knowing that self-esteem is not contingent on a smooth road, and 3) anticipating disappointments.

What worth is based on

- ▸ Worth as a person is not based on academic achievement or athletic performance. It is more process than outcome, hard work and effort rather than grades and scholarships.
- ▸ Resist comparisons to arbitrary standards or benchmarks.
- ▸ There is a difference between feeling discouraged and feeling unworthy.
- ▸ The self-evaluation process allows us to feel good when using our talents and doing what we can with abilities, rather than feeling bad if someone else does something better.
- ▸ Know the difference between core and peripheral issues: Core issues are their inner essence; peripheral issues are the day-to-day mistakes they make and the day-to-day disappointments they experience.
- ▸ Worth as a person is based more on inner values rather than how good we are at something.
- ▸ Teach them to view weak areas honestly, take stock, and know how to make a plan for self-improvement.

Self-esteem is not contingent on a smooth road

- ▸ Their opinion of themselves is more important than what others (teachers, coaches, and friends) think.
- ▸ Belonging is dessert, not the main course: Self-esteem does not have to float with how many friends kids have or if the "cool kids" let them in because it is their core that matters.
- ▸ We do not need approval from people we do not admire, and we do not admire people who tease or exclude.

> There will always be someone smarter, prettier, faster, better, and more talented.
> Forgive yourself; everybody is always working on something.
> Prepare for the world growing smaller, bumping into academic or athletic limits.

Anticipate disappointments

> It is acceptable to live between floors and ceilings. Floors symbolize "good enough" and ceilings symbolize perfection.
> Setbacks are common, so we should not be crushed by missed opportunities and dreams that evolve.
> We have value even when we make mistakes or suffer setbacks. Our value does not hinge on every single thing we do or that happens to us.
> Appreciate strengths even when confronted with weaknesses.
> Be comfortable with life as it is. Life just unfolds: it does not revolve around us.
> We adjust to the world, not the other way around.
> It is normal to not get everything we want. Prevent feelings of entitlement.
> We will always be part of a world that is imperfect and flawed.

2. EMOTIONAL CALIBRATION

The six skills children need to learn from us in order to be able to take care of their emotions are as follows: 1) language of feelings, 2) closure, 3) optimism, 4) thoughts precede feelings, 5) change and loss, and 6) sizing.

Language of feelings

> Look inward to understand feelings; that they are ours and are not completely caused by external events.

- Willing to share their feelings with us.
- Feelings pass: how we feel one moment will not be how we will always feel.
- Understand how feelings typically progress during transitions.

Closure

- Understand diminishing returns: that there is an upper limit to how much of our thoughts and feelings we can invest in something and have it be productive.
- Worrying is for when the sun is up. Problems seem bigger and scarier at night.
- Develop skills to avoid excessive worry.
- How to move on without getting caught in a ruminating (wheels spinning) trap.

Optimism

- "Viewing skills" are needed to deal with mistakes and disappointments.
- That we are more "can do" than "woe is me".
- Hard times are a normal part of life and always pass. Important lessons can be learned from hard times.
- To be kind to ourselves, forgive ourselves, and bounce back.
- Most people are good even though bad things happen.
- Learn to live with some evil in a mostly good world.

Thoughts precede feelings

- How we think precedes how we feel and how we act.
- Since we have choices in how we think we can influence how we feel.
- Life events alone do not determine how we must feel.
- How to be mindful and appreciative of the day; able to enjoy our days as they unfold without comparing them to how we wish they would be.

Change and loss

> ❯ To expect and be prepared for a life that includes both change and loss.
> ❯ Change and loss are a normal part of life. This includes friends moving away and getting cut from a team; as well as dealing with upsetting illness and death.
> ❯ Understand how the stages of grieving can help at times of change.
> ❯ To deal with academic and athletic losses and disappointments, and changes in friendships.

Sizing

> ❯ That we can influence our emotional reaction to life events.
> ❯ Choose to think about mistakes and disappointments in ways that make them easier to deal with and learn from throughout childhood.
> ❯ How to talk ourselves through difficult times so we can be more peaceful and less stressed.
> ❯ Know that we decide how big something is first, and then how we feel follows.

3. INTERPERSONAL SKILLS

The interpersonal skills are as follows: 1) boundaries and self-advocacy, 2) communication and conflict-resolution skills, 3) compassion, 4) trust, 5) personal growth process, 6) internal locus of control, and 7) stress management.

Boundaries and self-advocacy

> ❯ Encourage autonomy as they work towards independence.
> ❯ Be sensitive to enmeshment and dependency and how they affect relationships.
> ❯ Understand the confidence we have in them to do more of

their work and to solve more of their problems independently as they grow.

> Stand up for ourselves, protect our boundaries by speaking truth in direct and respectful ways, even if it hurts someone's feelings.

> Be assertive and powerful, not helpless or passive.

> Refuse to give our power away.

Communication and conflict-resolution skills

> Give and receive feedback.

> Understand the importance of talking directly to the person with whom you have an issue, rather than behind that person's back.

> The skills to connect with other children, ask questions, make small talk, and join in existing groups.

> Deal with difficult people and learn peacekeeping skills.

> See and take responsibility for their part of the conflict.

Compassion

> Learn to walk in another's shoes.

> Be sensitive to how the other person might be feeling.

> Develop an appreciation for the experience of others and how hard the world is for some people.

Trust

> Our "word" is how people come to know us as honest and dependable. Trust is important in a relationship. If trust is damaged by lying, it affects both the person saying and hearing the lie.

> Hard to know if they are telling us the truth the next time.

> Learn about loyalty and treachery. Be prepared for times when others are not trustworthy.

Personal growth process

> Acknowledge weak areas truthfully.
> Avoid the traps of denial, avoidance and minimizing.
> Learn to use our needs to set personal goals.
> Anticipate how we will be viewed.
> We are perfect exactly the way we are and we are always working on our personal goals. These two ideas coexist and need to be understood together.

Internal locus of control

> Look inward and rely on our inner voice and our own value system.
> Make good decisions by following our own lead rather than the lead of others.
> We are always responsible for what we do. Our behavior is not caused by an external event or what another child does.
> Develop immunity to peer pressure.

Stress management

> The importance of building a balanced life (nutrition, exercise, sleep, work and play).
> We feel better when we share concerns with people we trust.
> To be able to remember (at a stressful time), the other times when we dealt successfully with something similar.
> Resist fretting over things we cannot change.
> Friendships change and friendships end.
> It is important to cast a wide net and have "friend backups."
> To be wise about dating matters and avoid the trap of losing ourselves to others.
> Know what to do if they are worried about a friend who is at risk.

4. CONNECTED TO US

The two most important factors that lead to children staying closely connected to parents are as follows: 1) perceive us accurately as their reservoir of confidence, and 2) see discipline as consisting of logical consequences given by loving and forgiving parents.

Perceive us accurately as their reservoir of confidence

> - To know us as we truly are (rather than as we may appear at our weak moments).
> - We have their best interests at heart. See us as their reservoir of confidence.
> - Understand that we will honor their sovereignty as they grow up and that they are never a disappointment to us.
> - Understand their family of origin experience.

Logical consequences by loving and forgiving parents

> - That they are precious and loved at all times.
> - Mistakes will be forgiven but still warrant a consequence.
> - They can always tell us anything.
> - To keep their ears and hearts open to our advice and guidance.

5. WORK ETHIC

In order for children to develop a good work ethic they need to learn the following: 1) defer gratification and develop patience, 2) cooperate with authority, 3) the importance of education, and 4) the ability to work with anyone.

Defer gratification and develop patience

> - Be patient and considerate of others.
> - They do not get everything they need or desire the exact instant of their need or desire.

> Think before they act and anticipate natural consequences.
> Resist temptation.

Cooperate with authority

> There are more benefits to cooperating than not cooperating.
> The direct connection between the effort we put into something and its outcome.
> Parents have so much power that we never have to raise our voice or repeat ourselves.

Importance of education

> Develop "immunity" against underachievement.
> Develop the skills required for academic success (organization, managing time, looking ahead and setting interim deadlines).
> Teach an inner work ethic and the importance of being in charge of their responsibilities.

Ability to work with anyone

> Prepare them for a lifetime of work with all kinds of people.
> There is not one right way: Everyone is not like them.
> Know that there are many roads to adulthood and a wide range of acceptable lifestyles.

CONCLUSION

Teenagers who learn these skills navigate the social and academic pressures of high school better than the ones who do not, but the real challenge is that these skills are more easily learned years before they are needed. One parent said it helped her to remember that she was *always attending to both her children's short-term and long-term needs.* The short-term issues are easier to see (e.g., getting out of the house on time in the morning), but the long-term goals are the significant ones.

Some parents think dealing with the short-term constitutes all or most parenting. This is understandable with how busy families are. All we can do sometimes is get through the day. However, it is probably better to view the short-term as 20–25 percent of the job and the long-term as 75–80 percent. After all, how will our children be when they are 14, 16 and 18? Will they be resilient and optimistic? Will they make good decisions about friendships and dating? Will they adjust to life on a college campus? Will they still be talking and sharing with us and allowing us to help them when they are teenagers?

Parenting is making moments count. It is more than keeping the day running smoothly. There is so much to teach that we have to view every moment for its teaching opportunity and ask ourselves repeatedly: *"How may I use this, what can I teach?" Maybe there is something in every moment that can be taught and parenting well depends on finding it.*

Chapter 2

Celebrating Mistakes and Disappointments

First, let us clarify terms as they are used in this book. Anything children do that they should not do, and anything they do not do that they should, is a mistake. A list is provided (Appendix One) that includes behavior problems that are occasional, repetitive, even deliberate; and actions that are influenced by moods or lack of skills. Similarly, anything our children experience that we wish they did not, is a disappointment. A list of disappointments (Appendix Two) is provided that includes ordinary events (the plan for the day changes, you cannot drive them to a friend's house), world news (reports of wars, hurricanes, tsunamis) and significant losses (friends move away, pets die).

All children make mistakes and experience disappointments, nothing remarkable there. However, it is what we do next that is critical. It is easy to respond to a mistake with anger or impatience and end up with *too much distance* between parent and child. And with disappointments, it is easy to respond with hovering or rescuing and end up with *too little distance*. Both responses result in a missed moment.

Every mistake and each disappointment provide teaching opportunities. Mistakes seem "designed" for strengthening the parent-child connection, and disappointments are "perfect" for promoting resilience. Mistakes give us a perfect opportunity to demonstrate both our gentleness and our quickness to forgive. By our response we teach our children that they are not bad because they made a mistake—they made a mistake because that is how children learn. Celebrating mistakes for their teaching opportunity may be a peculiar concept at first, but it quickly becomes automatic.

If we handle their mistakes in a harsh and judgmental way, they may learn to hide their mistakes from us when they are older. One father heard himself say: "Don't you let me ever hear about something like this again." When he cooled off, he knew he *would want to hear* about "something like this" again. In fact, how else would he be able to help his children if he did not hear about *all* their mistakes over all the years?

Children are the same as us when it comes to admitting mistakes. We are more honest with people who understand us, forgive us, and help us learn from our mistakes, and we avoid admitting mistakes to people who are judgmental and quick to anger.

When your children are teenagers, they will predict your response to a current mistake by your responses to previous mistakes. Thinking about it this way, it is almost fortunate that we get all the mistakes of childhood to introduce and reintroduce ourselves to our children as approachable, forgiving and worthy of their adolescent journey. Without these mistakes, it would be harder for them to know how much we can handle, and how much we can forgive. One parent said in jest: "Aren't I the lucky one? My kids make more mistakes than anyone's!"

With disappointments, the desire to immediately do something to make them feel better comes from our love. But if we are not careful, the actions we take to make them feel better could rob them of a growth-promoting opportunity. If we throw ourselves into every disappointing moment, we might instill a sense of inadequacy. We do not have to panic when their road in life is not perfectly smooth. We can use the inevitable disappointments of childhood to teach the long-term goals.

We know growth comes from difficult times but it is hard to see that when our children are hurting. We cannot always prevent them from making mistakes or from experiencing disappointments, but we can remember that with so much to teach, *all kinds of moments are needed.* In fact, uneventful days are not particularly ripe for learning. When life is smooth, it may not be possible to teach about resilience or emotional calibration. Perhaps interpersonal skills are best learned at a time of sibling or friendship problems. *Children seem primed to learn important lessons at times of mistakes and disappointments.* And certain lessons are better learned at certain ages. One parent said it reminded her of a psychology class in college when she was studying how animals taught their young certain tasks at certain times. Our job is to view all the moments of childhood for the teaching opportunities they provide.

VIEWING PARENTING

Parents vary in how they view the "job description" of parenting. This is important because how we view parenting affects how we parent. The following exercise will explain this further.

Make a list of your "parent job description" and put the items in order of importance. This would be your personal conceptualization of parenting. How you feel as a parent will be influenced by this list. The list in Table Two was developed for parents who were in therapy because of family problems.

TABLE TWO—PRIORITIES OF PARENTING

1. Parenting is for the children—they need us or they would die.
2. Staying connected is more important than anything.
3. Each moment—no matter what—is a connection-strengthening opportunity.
4. Children's mistakes are gifts—they provide unique opportunities for teaching.
5. Expecting (and having a plan in place for) mistakes is our responsibility.
6. Every day is a day to enjoy our children—flawed as they are.
7. Knowing about their lives is critical: Keeping them talking to us is critical.
8. We can decide what battles to pick and what battles to skip.
9. To be safe in years to come, they need to feel safe with us now.
10. Faith development and instilling basic values of respect and responsibilities are crucial.
11. Children should always talk to their parents in appropriate ways.
12. A child's room should be clean and chores done with no procrastination.
13. Academic success—good progress reports and report cards.
14. Make sure children use their potential and do their best.
15. Prevent children from ever feeling sad or discouraged.
16. Make sure that children get things right the first time, or if they mess up, that they never repeat their mistake.
17. Success in sports, music or dance is important.
18. Getting them into the best college is critical.
19. Children are projects to be managed.
20. Children are a constant reflection of us, and our worth depends on their accomplishments.

Imagine this list in ascending order and in descending order. How differently would you think, feel and act with one list or the other? This exercise (although somewhat simplistic) was helpful with parents who had never examined their unstated assumptions about their role as parents. Many of us have an unwritten list and it helps to think about it and its origin.

Is your list your mother's, your father's or your neighbor's? Does it come from talk shows or magazine articles? Are you comfortable with it? Does it contribute to your ability to parent at your best even when your children are at their worst?

If two parents had the list in Table Two, but in reverse order, they would handle *every challenging moment* with their children completely differently. Nothing influences our day-to-day parenting more than our conceptualization of the job, and it is too important to leave unexamined.

WHAT IS UNIQUE TO THE PARENT ROLE?

Most parents are very dedicated, and Ellen was no exception. She was involved in every aspect of her children's lives and held them (and herself) to high expectations. This was stressful for all because her job description was endless. Ellen believed, as their mother, it was her job to ensure that they got along all the time, were assigned to teachers they liked, were never teased at recess, and got perfect grades. No wonder she was worn out! In therapy, her children worked on getting along with each other better, taking school seriously and getting good grades; and Ellen worked on seeing parenting in a new way so she could be calmer and more patient.

This new way required major changes because when Ellen felt responsible for so much, she had trouble being kind and loving. She was often tense; over-punishing for small mistakes, and crumbling when her children were upset. She had to reconfigure her parenting job description and unburden herself so she could focus on what *only she* could provide her children. *No one else can prepare children for adolescence.*

At its root, parenting is the relationship between two people—one parent and one child. Our job is to be the best parent we can be. Parenting is not the techniques we use, and even though we wish we could prevent their mistakes and grant them comfort and happiness at all times, that does not realistically belong in a parent job description.

Viewing childhood in a realistic way is necessary as well. Knowing how children typically behave at different ages, and accepting that progress is often slow, helps us view the challenging moments of childhood not only as normal but essential for the teaching opportunities they provide. When we are not realistic about how children typically behave at different ages, we are more likely to become angry, impatient or unnecessarily worried. Then, our reaction can make things worse rather than better.

Therapists consider the child's age whenever parents describe concerns. When children act in a way consistent with their age, it is less worrisome, even when the behavior is not welcomed. One colleague describes this type of behavior as "age-appropriate inappropriate" behavior. Parents still need to take action to help their children change, but they do not have to worry about what the behavior means. In the future, their children will be older and will most likely act the way children *that age* act. The light-hearted comment here is that they are continuously driving us crazy in new ways. The more serious and reassuring conclusion is that it is enough to simply look for opportunities to teach the long-term goals at times of age-appropriate inappropriate behavior.

For example, preschool children have trouble getting out of the house in the morning, have meltdowns in grocery stores and at family gatherings, act snotty or whiny and have trouble sharing. They may use their hands in an aggressive way, hitting or shoving another child. There may be a big fuss when it is time to put toys away or brush teeth. And 3- and 4-year-olds, who have terrific lives and love their parents with all their heart and soul will say, "I hate you," or even "I hate myself," from time to time. Having trouble falling asleep and being reluctant to try new things occur frequently. These problems are best viewed as normal for the age. Therefore, we do not have to be very concerned.

As children move into their first few years of school, sibling rivalry continues or even intensifies, and they can still have trouble playing with their friends. They might have trouble separating from us in the morning, feel nervous if we have to travel on a business trip or panic at bedtime. Six and 7-year-olds can be mean to pets or say unkind things about their teachers, coaches, instructors or ministers. They lie, especially in an attempt to avoid a consequence. They try to manipulate us, turning mother against father if it works to their advantage. "Naughty" words are learned, chores are forgotten, and power struggles begin.

Third- 4th- and 5th-graders struggle with behavior that seems like a lack of respect for themselves, their parents, rules, and expectations. And parents often worry that if they are acting this way at this age, what will they be like when they are teenagers? The humor at this age can be off-color (bathroom jokes), and they might take something that does not belong to them. Task completion is a challenge. Homework and chores still require supervision, but reminders are resented. Ten-year-olds can complain about feeling bored when they are surrounded by things they could be doing. Doors are slammed, eyes are rolled, and their tone of voice can be sarcastic. However, what they do at 9 and 10 is not as powerful a predictor of what they will do at 15 or 16, as how *we respond to the challenges of 9 and 10.*

The years after fifth grade and before high school can be joyful or tortuous for parents. Defiance and power struggles seem to be everywhere. Eleven- and 12-year-olds experiment with different styles of dress, choice of friends, even different identities. They may act as if they view us as irrelevant at best, "dumber than dirt" at worst. Their organization skills are still poorly developed, with time management problems and difficulty keeping track of school projects.

Inappropriate conversations or messages might be overheard or intercepted. Whether these years are joyous or tortuous depends less on how *they* behave and more on how *we* understand their behavior.

To be the best "us" we can be with our children, we need to stay calm when they are acting their age even when it is not pleasant. If we have not learned this skill yet, we can learn it now. Not only will our children benefit from this during their childhood, but they will continue to benefit when they are adults. The next chapter focuses on how to be at our best at all times, even when our children are challenging.

Chapter 3

Viewing Moments

Many parents see teaching opportunities on less stressful days but not on more stressful days. Unfortunately, life seems to have no shortage of stressful days! Our days are filled with appointments, childcare, driving to activities, "to do" lists and pressure from work; in addition to children's mistakes and disappointments.

Sometimes it seems we could hold it together "if only" there were no surprises. With our plates full, we might view their mistakes as the last straw and react poorly. Parenting at our best at those times is helped by learning to view non-family stress in ways that prevent our plates from filling up.

The times of mistakes and disappointments will carry their own stress. If that is added to days already filled with the stress of unreasonable bosses, self-centered colleagues, and traffic jams, that is an unsettling combination.

Yet our feelings at the end of the day are not entirely due to the day itself. Bosses can be unreasonable and traffic impossible, but they bother us more on some days than others. The explanation for how *we can feel differently* when dealing with similar stressors is something *in us,* rather than something *outside of us.*

With our bosses, traffic or anything our children do, we choose how to view moments. *Our emotional response is not first and is not completely the result of what happened.* The choice we make about viewing magnifies or moderates our emotional reaction. This choice seems immediate, almost without awareness. But once we start paying attention to it we can influence the viewing choice we make.

Unreasonable bosses might be viewed as insecure and annoying but not worthy of aggravation. They have power over us economically but maybe we can prevent them from having power over how much sleep we lose. Same with traffic. None of us look forward to a twenty-minute trip taking forty minutes, but we can view it as inconvenient rather than catastrophic.

While it may initially seem unlikely to *change how you feel by how you think,* it is actually quite possible. It takes practice, but we can practice every hour of every day, without taking any time from any of our responsibilities. We can even practice in traffic! Maybe the extra twenty minutes becomes valuable time to be just with ourselves, or time for music or news. We can view it as a chance to stay current with our reading by listening to recorded books.

Our viewing skills will never be as important as when *our children are our stress.* By practicing these skills throughout the day, while we are breathing in and breathing out, we learn to modify the external event and its power over how we feel. The more practice the better.

PRACTICE

Practicing our viewing skills helps us stay calmer during stress and helps us find the teaching opportunities. The following stories help illustrate this point.

One parent said she used her alarm clock as a reminder. She started therapy with her 6th-grade son, Johnny, because he seemed to be drifting, less willing to talk with her about his day, perhaps even a little depressed. After just a few sessions, he had convinced her that it was not that at all, it was just that she was so busy and irritable lately. As soon as he said it, she knew he was right. However, she thought she had no choice in how she felt.

Her first thoughts were anxious ones: "I hope the day goes smoothly." "Will I get everything done that needs to get done?" "I better remind Johnny that he has a dentist appointment after school today." She sounded as if she woke up in a three-point stance, preparing herself to run a race or charge into the other team's offensive line. Gradually, she worked on replacing those frantic thoughts with thoughts that were more reassuring. "Today will be busy but enough will get done, it always does." "I'm going to get my walk in at lunch time no matter how busy the day is." It took a while, but slowly, she began to be more relaxed and her son benefited as well.

Sometimes we set a trap for ourselves by hoping for days without surprises. Naturally we want days to go smoothly and according to our plan, but how many days are actually like that? It is different to start the day expecting it to be however it will be—assuming surprises. While it is great when a day unfolds exactly the way we hoped, we cannot count on that happening too often. It is better to be pleasantly surprised when a day unexpectedly unfolds smoothly than to be overly stressed when a day does not.

Families move around a lot, and this story comes from a father who moved to Minnesota from Texas. If you live in a region like Minnesota that gets four seasons, you know that a 30-degree day in September elicits a strong reaction. People compare it to the recent 70-degree days and put on warm sweaters and jackets. However, in January, after temperatures in the single digits, a 30-degree day feels almost like a heat wave. It is the same 30-degrees. This father really was shocked twice: at how cold the 30-degree day seemed in September and again at how warm it seemed in January. How external events (in this case a 30-degree day) are experienced depends on us.

Ordinary traffic, weather, even car problems, permit practice. A parent told me that she took her new car to the dealer for its first routine maintenance. When it was done, she picked it up, drove off and saw smoke pouring out of the engine. She was still in the neighborhood (and was safe), called them, got towed back and waited for the car to be worked on again. The mechanic forgot to put one of the caps back on. She had her day changed unexpectedly and used the unwanted time at the car dealer's to study for a class. That night at dinner, she used her experience to talk about the choice she made about how to view the inconvenience. She told her children that instead of comparing her day to the day she thought she was going to have, she kept thinking about how lucky she was to have a new car, a cell phone to call the dealer, to be safe and healthy: "I just could not work up the energy to feel all that bad about it. I canceled a few things and read my book."

If you were a baseball player and somebody told you that you could practice hitting and fielding every minute of every day, you would assume that your skills would steadily improve. It is the same with us. We can practice viewing skills every minute of every day and get better as well. If we are stuck in the slow line at the grocery store, we can view it as a minor irritation and as a chance to work on our patience. If drivers cut us off, we can view them as pitiful and not worthy of an emotional reaction.

One parent told me she liked the idea of practicing throughout the day and since life with children is so stressful, she decided that it was a blessing that life was as stressful as it is. How else would she get all the practice she needed to be calm, patient and forgiving with her children!

THOUGHTS PRECEDE FEELINGS

The same traffic jam can be more aggravating to one driver than to another or to the same person on two different days. The same 30-degree day can be felt as warmer or cooler. This is because *thoughts precede feelings and thoughts can be replaced or modified.* Imagine how the woman's day would have been if she viewed the smoky car differently. What if she talked with her children at dinner about how her whole day had been ruined, the meetings she had to cancel, and how even the next day was going to be affected because she was now so far behind. That would be a very different lesson from the same external event. Instead, she opted for: "This is what I did with my less-than-perfect day."

It is not so different in parenting. The external events, the challenging moments with our children, do not have to cause us to feel any particular way. In fact, two parents will often view the same type of event in different ways. One might get very angry, one might be slightly bothered. Subtle differences in parenting repeated over many years can lead to very different scenarios during adolescence.

CHANGING HOW WE VIEW MOMENTS

It is difficult but important work to be in charge of how we view moments. The first step is often asking: "How do I choose to view this, and what thoughts will help me do that?" Parents often say, after a few therapy sessions, that they understand "this whole viewing thing," but explain that they are just too quick-tempered or too worried about their children's future to be as calm and patient as this approach requires. Changing how we view moments of family life requires deliberate effort because all of our experiences, our role models when we were growing up, and our beliefs about childhood, influence how we view those moments. What is not always clear at first is that *the viewing skills can help us be calm and patient.*

Just as we reduce our stress by not expecting every day to be perfectly smooth, we can expect our children to make mistakes and experience disappointments. We can decide that these are the *joys of parenting:* the tantrums, the forgotten chores and the rude backtalk. We can help our children learn from these mistakes and show them how we handle stress at the same time.

Instead of comparing a moment to how we think it should be, we ask ourselves: "What can I learn about my child from this mistake or disappointment? How may I use this moment? What can I teach?" The next chapter discusses blind spots, the barriers to viewing moments in helpful ways, but a few examples here will illustrate the basic premise.

When children behave inappropriately, it is tempting to compare them to how they should be behaving and then feel annoyed. With practice, we stay with the moment and do what we can. If they speak to us rudely, we give them a consequence. We can say, "That hurts my ears, and when my ears hurt, you cannot have a friend over." We handle it better when we are unhurt, unworried and unstressed by their words, and we manage that by viewing their remarks as mistakes, a normal and inevitable part of childhood.

And if this same child speaks to us rudely in the morning AND does not put their toys away in the afternoon (AND they tell us they brushed their teeth, but the toothbrush is dry, AND they tease their younger brother), we resist comparing their behavior to the behavior we would prefer. Instead, we teach what we can and avoid making things worse by our reaction.

When stuck about how to view a moment, ask: *"How else could this be viewed?"* Even when there seems to be only one way, there are always several. By looking for the thoughts that are influencing our viewing, we are able to make changes.

There are options in how to view our children's mistakes. We can decide they are "stuck" for a while. Or, they are handling stress poorly. A sense of humor and humility will help: "Of course they are flawed—they have us for parents!" At certain ages, children will be rude and obnoxious, at other ages, whiny and forgetful. A mother of seven wholeheartedly believed that children are "knuckleheads" until they are done being "knuckleheads." A well-developed discipline plan (Chapter Six) will help them change as fast as they can change.

What about mistakes that children make over and over for many months? Parents often stay calm the first few times but then get frustrated. This might be because they view the problem as lasting longer than it should, which is a comparison to an ideal. Viewing the problem this way, the parent might make the consequences bigger and longer-lasting, risking unnecessary hurt feelings. Alternatively, if a parent believes that children make mistakes until they learn what they need to learn, it is easier to stay calm. We give consequences, the behavior changes as fast as it can, and we are more successful in how we handle ourselves.

Sometimes our stress comes from the unrealistic expectation that children's progress should be fast and without setbacks. A more realistic expectation is that growth takes time. Some problems are revisited many times, with lessons not fully learned until months or years later. Perhaps the most important goals take the most repetitions. We do not have to become impatient, and our viewing skills help us stay relaxed and confident.

We have a choice in how we view their pace of change. We do not have to set a mental timer for how many weeks or months the problem should be allowed to linger. Adults do not change on a dime. Sometimes it is easier to forgive ourselves or our adult friends for repeated mistakes than it is our own children. One father came up with a creative way to remember this. All he had to do was think of his New Year's resolutions and how they still include the same goals since before he was even married (eat better, exercise, call his parents more often), and that helped him hang in there when his children changed slowly. And of course anyone who is married knows how long it takes their spouse to change!

It helps to view our children as being exactly who they have to be every moment of every day—given their life story to date, current circumstances, and having loving but flawed parents. We help them without judging. Many people believe things happen for a reason or believe they can bring meaning to an event by their actions. In the first case, when children make mistakes or experience disappointments, it is up to the parent to find the good in what is happening. In the second case, parents use what is happening for the children's best interests.

VIEWING MOMENTS AND PARENTING

Here are two examples that demonstrate the power of viewing, one dealing with how a parent views his daughter, the other how a child views a problem at recess.

Even though George's daughter was heading for college in the fall, he asked her to come to therapy with him a few times that summer. She reluctantly agreed, telling him everything was fine and that he was being overly concerned. They had always been close, but lately she seemed evasive with him, as if she was hiding something. When he called for the first appointment, he was viewing her behavior as likely due to a boyfriend matter or perhaps decisions she was making on weekends. As it turned out, she was fine, just preparing herself for life in college. When this became clear, he was able to view her behavior, unchanged by therapy, as part of her process of convincing both of them that she was an adult now—on her own and ready to move out. Seeing her behavior in this way helped him worry less.

George's full-moon story is a great reminder about the power of viewing. He noticed how the full moon looked huge on the horizon when it was rising and how later that night it looked smaller when it was directly overhead—not later in the month, but later that same night. He knew enough astronomy to know that it was not the size of the moon or its distance from earth that had changed, only the way he was looking at it at each time. On the horizon, the moon could be compared to trees or buildings, but there was nothing to compare it to when it was overhead. It helped George remember how much better he felt after he changed how he was viewing his daughter during her summer before college, even though she had not changed at all.

The "viewing" step can dramatically affect how we feel, how we react to the stress in our lives and how we parent. It allows us to adjust our feelings even when the stressful moment has not changed.

Now think about a 4th-grade boy who comes home from school crying because he was alone at recess. There are two separate, but connected, viewing steps here. If parents view this as an unfortunate but potentially growth-promoting event, the child can learn that while it is upsetting, it is not devastating. The child can be reminded that he does not always include every other child at recess either, that he had kids to play with yesterday, and probably will tomorrow. With this approach, the child begins to learn how to view disappointments. If parents view an upsetting day at recess as a significant trauma, perhaps as a sign of unkind children or unsupportive school personnel, the child may develop a sense of despair, pessimism, or entitlement.

ONE CHILD, TWO REACTIONS

Frank and Diane brought their 11-year-old son, Joel, to therapy because of the tension between Frank and Joel. Interestingly, Diane and Joel were getting along fine. Frank said it made him furious when Joel rolled his eyes back in his head and made a certain dismissive sound when Frank was talking. Frank wanted Joel to stop rolling his eyes and making that sound.

Frank was in a high-level position at work, supervising many in a Fortune 500 company in Minneapolis. Nobody at work rolled their eyes or sneered at him. In addition, he did not have younger siblings when he was growing up, had not done any babysitting, and was not familiar with how obnoxious and self-absorbed 11-year-olds can be. Diane was an excellent disciplinarian, tolerated none of the rudeness, gave consequences, but did not lose her temper.

Here were two parents dealing with the same child's inappropriate behavior. When Frank was able to view his son's behavior merely as a problem in need of a consequence, the tension began to subside. That is, by changing how he viewed the inappropriate behaviors, he no longer thought they were serious signs of disrespect that could get worse over time. He became calmer and less likely to lose his temper. Instead of focusing on what his son was doing and then reacting without insight, he turned his attention to his part of the relationship. He said the turning point for him was this story:

Two 8-year-old boys get into trouble at school for shouting and hitting. One says: "He called me a bad name so I called him one back." The other boy says: "He made me mad so I hit him."

Fathers, like 8-year-old boys, have to be responsible for their actions, and they cannot blame their sons for how they react to eye rolling. It does not work very well for adults to argue that their children make them lose their temper! Viewing the behavior as inappropriate but not catastrophic helped Frank stay more in control. Since Diane was viewing the behavior differently, she was able to react differently.

Small decisions about how to view our children, repeated thousands of times over eighteen years, produce a cumulative effect.

Imagine two sets of parents with 10-year-old boys who are not pulling their weight at school or around the house. In one family, the parents give consequences calmly and the problem gradually improves. The other parents are more intense, use louder voices, and contribute to escalating family scenes. The difference is not in the child but in how the child's behavior is viewed. Over many years, one boy will be more closely connected with his parents than the other boy.

BLESS THE ROAD YOU ARE ON

We work with the day as it unfolds, and we try not to compare it to the day we wish was unfolding. It will only hurt us to compare the traffic jam with an open road. It will not change the traffic. We start from "I'm in traffic, what can I do with this?" We accept the moment as it is and rely on our viewing skills. With our children, we work with them as they are and help them with whatever they need. One mother liked the phrase: "Bless the road you're on" because it referred to traffic as well as the journey she was on with her children.

Accepting things as they are does not prevent us from working for change. We do not make excuses for our children's unacceptable behavior, and we do not hesitate to discipline, but we discipline without causing unnecessary interpersonal stress.

SAME KIDS, DIFFERENT DAYS

Imagine yourself on two very different types of days. One day you come home after a terrific day (compliment from the boss, successful project completed, favorite team won the big game), another day you arrive home burdened with imminent deadlines and difficult colleagues. On both days you come home to whiny, ungrateful children demanding that you do something for them "right now." It is likely that you will view the whiny children differently on the two days.

A father can come home to a messy house and stay calm or lose his temper. If he believes that children should always be tidy (keep their room clean, pick up after themselves without reminders), he will be aggravated. If he wants them to be tidy but expects them to "forget" occasionally, he will still have a messy house at times, but he will not get upset. He might say to himself: "Now I get to help them with this problem." And he might say to them, in a soft and reassuring voice: "Chores didn't get done tonight, so early bed. Let's take care of the room because it still needs to be picked up."

The difference is both small and big. Viewing the problem as an ordinary part of parenting is different from viewing it as a sign of disrespect by irresponsible children.

One parent felt so discouraged about her ability to stay calm and loving when her children were being difficult that she asked in jest: "What drugs would I have to be on in order to be able to stay that calm?" The answer to staying calm is in how we view childhood and how we view parenting.

For example, we will feel one way if we think children should always follow our rules and another way if we believe that children are "works in progress," with mistakes expected. The aggravations of parenting can help strengthen the connection if we view them as opportunities to introduce and reintroduce ourselves to our children as their biggest fans, rather than their biggest critics. Children who are strong-willed and challenging for many years can be close to their parents and absolutely fine during adolescence depending on how their parents handled the difficult moments. The next chapter discusses the blind spots that can interfere with how we view moments.

Chapter 4

Blind Spots

We parent at our best when we are connected with our children and able to view moments peacefully. Anything that interferes with this is called a blind spot because it prevents us from seeing something that is right in front of us. By paying attention to the times we struggle with our parenting we find out where we need to change.

There is so much that affects us when we are parenting. We bring our whole lives to every moment with our children:

- Our role models—what we learned from our parents and others we have known. What we learned about childhood before we became parents—from siblings, other children in the neighborhood, or babysitting.
- Memories of adolescence.
- How familiar we are with developmental expectations at different ages.
- Life circumstances in general—how careers are going, dealing with an ill parent.
- Our own midlife issues.

How we view parenting moments depends on us, not on our children. When we react it may be because of our buttons, triggers or a personality characteristic, rather than what they are doing. We want to pay close attention so we can learn what we can from each event. What set us off? How were we viewing it?

Ask parents about regretted moments with their children and you will get an earful. Some overreact to whining or complaining. Others lose their temper if they are being ignored by their children. When there is a history of significant losses, parents can worry so much about the future that they parent poorly in the present. Some nag so much about homework that they annoy their children and contribute to future problems with underachievement.

USING OUR BLIND SPOTS TO CHANGE HOW WE PARENT

Parents start a notebook as part of family therapy to keep track of the regretted times. This clarifies that it is not their children's actions causing their response. After all, two parents can respond differently to a situation depending on how they are viewing it. And the same parent can respond with some variation on different days.

A DAY AT THE BEACH

Here are two versions of a day at the beach with children. First, a day with a clear view, then, the same day with blind spots. Imagine that Kathy, 35, has a day off from work and is spending a summer day with her three children. Nick is 4, Joni is 7 and Chuck is 9. She had a good night's sleep, they are all healthy and the bills are paid. Her husband comes home from work that evening, and she tells him about three challenging parts of the day:

> ▸ Nick was not ready to leave the beach when it was time and had a meltdown.
> ▸ Joni was pouting and whiny all afternoon, talking about how it is not fair that Nick does not have to do any chores yet, and Chuck gets to spend an overnight with his friend.
> ▸ Chuck did not put his toys away when he was supposed to, and gave Kathy a disrespectful sneer when she asked.

WITH A CLEAR VIEW

On this day, Kathy was able to see the teaching opportunities in these three moments. Nick needed to see that his tantrum was not going to influence their decision to leave the beach, and she was able to discipline him calmly. She was not too worried about the tantrum because she knew 4-year-olds have trouble with transitions. In addition, even though there were people she knew at the beach, she did not think they were judging her, and she was not worried about what they were thinking of her as a parent.

Joni's negativity did not bring Kathy down at all—she was able to be loving and forgiving because she knew sibling rivalry is an inevitable part of having three children in six years. She did what she always does: Gave Joni a warning, then a two-minute time-out in her room, telling her that "it hurts Mommy's ears to hear all that complaining" and "as soon as you get all that whining out of you, we can play a game of cards before dinner."

Kathy does not appreciate having to repeat herself so she tries not to (especially with a 9-year-old). When Chuck refused to put his toys away, Kathy simply put them in a box and put them away for a few days. She did not repeat the request and she did not make a big scene. Chuck will miss his toys, and he will not get them back until she gives them back. Kathy is not viewing this as a predictor of how he will handle future responsibilities, and she is not trying to figure out what his "sneer" might mean psychologically.

Small moments, well handled. Parenting is a series of small moments, and the parent-child interaction is an evolving dance where each dancer's actions affect the other's actions. The bigger problems in later years (17-year-olds coming home after curfew, hanging out with the wrong crowd) are influenced by how we handle all the meltdowns at the beach and all the toys not put away.

THE SAME DAY WITH BLIND SPOTS

How might Kathy have handled herself on a more typical (less idyllic) day? Imagine she worked until late afternoon before going to the beach. Her husband had an evening meeting, so she was on her own for the dinner and bedtime shifts. Her mother had some medical tests recently and the results would arrive today or tomorrow.

When Nick has his meltdown at the beach, Kathy might be less calm and patient. She might feel embarrassed when she sees her neighbor. Her mind might start to race with thoughts that add to her stress.

> ▸ "Doesn't Nick appreciate that I was able to get him to the beach at all?"
> ▸ "How am I going to get dinner started if we don't leave right this minute?"
> ▸ "Chuck should really know better at his age. He should be helping me with the younger kids, not making more work for me all the time."
> ▸ "And Joni's whining! The sound of it drives me crazy. If she doesn't stop whining right this minute, my head will explode."

It is not just what our children do, it is what we do next. That is why it is important to look inward to find anything that might block our views of parenting and childhood.

Think about the times you do not handle well or when you cannot find the teaching opportunities. You might hear yourself say:

> ▸ "He made me so mad that I lost my temper."
> ▸ "How can I be calm when he makes me so worried?"
> ▸ "If she acts this way at 7, what is she going to be like at 15?"
> ▸ "They should have realized that I had a rough day and cooperated better."

Parenting at our best (even when our children are challenging) requires insight and self-awareness, and these internal comments suggest a lack of both. This chapter will help you identify your blind spots so you will be able to see what to teach at all times.

OBSERVE WITHOUT REACTING

First, pay attention to your experience throughout the day. *What happens to you and what happens inside of you?* Be careful about the tendency to assume that your first reaction is the only one possible. *Question your first response.* How we parent is not determined by what they just did. After all, if you had 1,000 parents dealing with a disrespectful 10-year-old (or a bad grade), some would be frantic and angry, others controlled and deliberate in their response. Some parents talk about losing sleep when their children have friendship problems, others feel a little upset but believe such problems are an inevitable part of childhood. There are always choices in how to view moments.

THE FIRST SESSION

Psychologists sometimes describe the first session of family therapy as a finger-pointing session, because parents point to what their children have been doing. Towards the end of the first session (or as soon as possible), the focus shifts to what strategies the parents have tried, and whether they have been in control of themselves during the difficult times. The pace of progress in therapy is often determined by whether the parent views their children's behavior as causing their response.

Parents who view their own behavior as caused by their children's behavior sometimes view their behavior in other parts of life as caused by external events as well. This external locus of control can be accompanied by a reluctance to look inward. The willingness to look inward and accept responsibility for what we do as parents helps us parent peacefully. Without this we are merely reacting. We might get angry when they make a mistake. We might worry when they are disappointed. We might be impatient when they are not changing fast enough.

Without insight into our blind spots, our children could be hurt more by our parenting than by what we are trying to help them with in the first place. Parents who find it hard to start this insight work sometimes say it is because they are new to talking about relationships in general, not only in the parent-child relationship. One father told me that he had virtually no experience talking about relationships, even though he was in his late twenties, had been married for seven years and had dated throughout adolescence. He needed to be reassured that, even though occasionally hard, it is important work and it can be done.

Do not be discouraged if practice is needed. Resist the idea that external events control how we feel. Just as we have a choice in how we feel when we are stuck in traffic, we have a choice in how we feel when we are with our children. We do not have to be annoyed when our children are annoying and we do not have to be provoked when they are provoking us.

This is where the real work in therapy begins, when parents stop looking at their children's behavior as the cause of their own behavior. It might take three or four sessions, sometimes longer, but there comes a point where the parent says: "I'm here to talk about me today, not my children. I'm not able to parent the way I want to and it's not because of what they are doing."

This chapter is a compilation of the work parents begin at that moment when they start to consider their own blind spots. Instead of focusing on the changes the parents want their children to make, they try to learn what is interfering with their ability to see their children and their children's needs clearly. When they identify their blind spots and are then able to be in the moment with their children, they are able to see how best to use the moments for teaching. *All the moments,* even the ones described as mistakes and disappointments.

The blind spots are presented here for you to read through once and then refer back to as you read subsequent chapters. Just as in therapy, the most important issues have to be revisited many times, and you may find that you learn more about your own blind spots after several readings. They are organized into four general areas: 1) worrying, 2) judging, 3) intruding, and 4) hesitating. Each blind spot is listed in Table Three and then described in more detail in the pages that follow.

TABLE THREE—BLIND SPOTS

1. The Worrying Blind Spots

> ➤ Overly Emotional
> ➤ Low Tolerance for Conflict
> ➤ Over-psychologizing
> ➤ Sizing
> ➤ Projecting Linearly

2. The Judging Blind Spots

> ➤ Invisible Rulebooks
>> ◆ Comparisons
>> ◆ Appear As If Our Love is Conditional
> ➤ Expecting Payback
> ➤ Inaccurately Inserting Intent

3. The Intruding Blind Spots

> ➤ Views Parenting as Cloning
> ➤ Myth of the Smooth Road
> ➤ Poor Listener When Helping
> ➤ Over-helps

4. The Hesitating Blind Spots

> ➤ Worships Their Children
> ➤ Lacks Confidence in Their Parenting
> ➤ Naïve

As parents learn about these fifteen blind spots in therapy, they begin to pay attention at home, between sessions, to the times when they did not handle a situation well. They bring those stories back to therapy and significant progress can be made. You can try this without therapy. Observe whether you are affected by one blind spot more than the others. Look for patterns. Perhaps one blind spot interferes more when you are with one child rather than another. Maybe your children's disappointments elicit certain blind spots and their mistakes elicit others.

Once parents understand the kind of mistakes and disappointments that are difficult for them to handle well, they are able to work on their viewing skills. The idea is to reduce the power situations hold over their feelings and how they parent. It is exciting to watch parents use this information about themselves to change how they handle similar moments in the future.

For example, if parents learn they react poorly to certain mistakes when their children are young, they also learn that they might react poorly to similar mistakes when their children are older. Instead of viewing the children's behavior at one age as the predictor of their behavior when they are older, it makes more sense to view *our reaction at one time as the predictor of our reaction* when they are older. This is less confusing than it sounds at first and will become clearer as you read further. For now, just remember that our blind spots are influenced by how we view moments, and what leads us to parent one way when our children are young, may lead us to parent that way when they get older. But the best part of this approach is we can change how we view moments and change how we parent.

To help you decide if a blind spot has been interfering in your parenting, each one comes with a list of questions. This section is labeled: "Does this blind spot affect you?" Each list of questions is followed by a section called: "What to do about it." It is probably best to read the entire chapter once, make marks next to the ones that are descriptive of *your* parenting, and when you refer back to this section, pay the most attention to *your* blind spots.

1. THE WORRYING BLIND SPOTS

Parenting is all about worry, and while it is impossible to eliminate, we can minimize its impact on our parenting. In fact, many of us worry the most about the less likely scenarios and not enough about the more likely ones. For example, parents sometimes explain a frustrated or angry response by saying they were "just so worried." However, if the worrying controls us and prevents us from handling ourselves well, we might need to worry more about that than what was originally worrying us about our children's behavior.

One mother was worried about her 5-year-old son because he was having trouble saying goodbye to her in the drop-off lane at school. She said he looked sad and kept asking her what she would be doing all day. He was focusing on the day being too long and how much he was going to miss her. Looking back on it, he was having a slight adjustment problem to all-day kindergarten, but her reaction was not helping.

This scene brought her back to losses she had experienced as a child. Her parents divorced when she started school, and she talked about the tension (overheard telephone conversations, the "handoff" at the end of a weekend visit) that made her sensitive to loss issues. She knew *he* was fine after they separated (the teacher reassured her about this many times), but *her* tears made the separation harder than it needed to be.

Parents are allowed to be sensitive to loss issues (many of us are), but without insight, our relationships with our children might be negatively affected. What if the 5-year-old says goodbye without a care? Or a 5th-grader comes home from school and goes straight to his room? Or a 9th-grader wants to spend all her time with friends? These normal transitions can trigger our loss issues. Thinking about parenting as continuous grieving resonates with many parents. Even though no one is dying, we mourn the endings (e.g., breastfeeding and diapers) and the beginnings (first day of school, first sleepover at a friend's house), because they are reminders of how fast time passes.

The stages of grieving (denial, anger, bargaining, depression, acceptance) that we go through at times of loss apply to parenting as well.

A colleague (a high school principal) once said parents in *denial* parent as if their children were three years younger than they actually are. Her helpful observation was about the parents who need to be "dragged kicking and screaming into the present." Often, this is because of their reluctance to admit that children are always moving away from parents. Children, however, are usually very excited about being as grownup as possible and are eager for the next part of their journey. If we are not careful, we may inadvertently insult our children by helping too much or talking to them as if they were still younger:

> ▸ We should not tie their shoelaces one day longer than they need us to.
> ▸ We should not remind them about their homework after 9 or 10.
> ▸ We should allow them the joy of waking up to a non-human alarm clock as soon as possible, certainly before sixth grade.

Thinking about these issues as possibly related to the "denial of loss" stage of grieving can be helpful. We enjoyed being the center of their world and may have trouble letting go of that role in their lives.

Some parental *anger* might be related to this second stage of grief. Prior to adolescence (think fourth or fifth grade) children begin testing limits in small ways, and being defiant in ways they never were before. It makes sense that we might mourn the younger child who would have never treated us this way. If this fits, you can talk with your child about how you "miss the way we used to get along" with a sad tone, rather than an angry one. If a consequence is needed, you can give one and address the issue without anger.

Bargaining may appear when limits begin to intrude in our

children's lives. There might be a sense of loss if children struggle with academics or athletics. There might be more time on the bench than on the playing field, or homework might take longer than ever, and the grades earned may be lower than in years past. Parents who understand their own feelings as part of a grieving process will be better able to avoid blaming a teacher for teaching too fast, or for giving too much homework, or blaming the coach for favoring the other players.

Depression might be too strong a word to describe the empty feeling parents sometimes have when their children's center shifts away from them and towards their friends. We know they are developing their autonomy and independence, but we might miss the incredibly important relationship we enjoyed for so many years. The familiar intimacy will be replaced with something that has not arrived yet, something new and unknown. And even though they have not done anything purposefully to hurt us, we may feel hurt anyway, just by their movement towards their own future.

There is peace in *accepting* the role that grieving plays in parenting. They are ours for a very short time. When we think about the day-to-day changes in this way, we accept the inevitable losses of parenting. In time, they are off to college and their own marriages and families, and for now, we try not to let our sensitive feelings about loss negatively affect our parenting.

Overly Emotional

Each of us was a person before we became a parent, and we continue to be individuals after our children are born. As you recall, parenting is basically the relationship between us and our children, and worrying can impair how we pull off our half of the relationship. Our experiences may have led us to be thin-skinned and easily hurt. We might carry our own sensitivity to loss and overreact emotionally. It may look like we are responding to our children and their moments, but our entire history is there at the same time. Here are the flags that might help you decide if this is one of your blind spots:

Does this blind spot affect you?

> Are you generally fearful (not just about parenting), harboring significant anxiety about the future? Do you often worry and make things worse by your reaction rather than better?
> As your children move through their stages and become more and more independent, are you terribly saddened by a sense of eventual loss? Is it very stressful to think of their need for you decreasing as they become more autonomous?
> When you sense that your children are about to make a mistake or experience a disappointment, do you overreact in a way that is not helpful?
> Do your experiences with loss and grief affect how you parent at sensitive times?
> Is it hard for you to comfort your children when they have friendship problems because you get so emotional?
> Have you ever felt embarrassed when a teacher called about a school problem, imagining that the teacher is being critical of you?
> Does it "hurt so much" when your children talk to you unkindly? Do you wear your heart on your sleeve, often taking things too personally?
> Do you resist the idea that adversity and disappointments can strengthen your children, wishing you could somehow prevent them from ever feeling uncomfortable in any way?
> Is there a chance that you are inadvertently teaching your children to be thin-skinned by modeling that everything is a big deal?

What to do about it:

▸ Remember: The cause of our worry is not necessarily "out there." Just because we feel worried does not mean there is something to worry about. Even when there is cause to worry, parenting with worry does not necessarily help.

▸ We parent better when we pay attention to the worry, observe it, and not react right away.

▸ We fly when worried, drive when worried, and we *can parent calmly* when worried. When we worry, it may have more to do with the past or the future rather than the present.

▸ How would we parent differently if we were not so worried? Would it be easier to forgive when they say something unkind and easier to let go of our uncomfortable feelings as well?

▸ They need us to be their reservoir of confidence. Children might back away from us if we are too much of a nuisance.

▸ Conserving our parenting resources means always intervening for health and safety reasons but not to prevent every disappointment.

▸ While something may be hurtful to us, it is not necessarily hurtful for our children.

▸ Reassure yourself that even though children act in upsetting ways, things will be fine if you do not get too upset. Strategies to deal with what is happening are better than wallowing in the emotional pain with them.

Low Tolerance for Conflict

Some parents have thick skin, while some are quite easily hurt by day-to-day conflicts with children. The ideal is not to be unaffected by the angry words or the power struggles that are an inevitable part of life with children. It is just harder to be kind and compassionate if we hurt about every little thing. Here are flags to help you decide if this is one of your blind spots:

Does this blind spot affect you?

> In general, do you get very upset with minor conflicts with adults (co-workers, relatives, neighbors)?
> Is your day practically ruined if one of your children speaks to you disrespectfully?
> Does your confidence get shaken when others are annoyed with you or dissatisfied with something you have done?
> Have you ever wondered about whether you have an especially high need to have the approval of others?
> Do you feel embarrassed over relatively small events (e.g., someone notices your children acting inappropriately in a department store or at a family gathering)?
> Are the day-to-day conflicts (getting the children to put their coats in the closet, hang the towel on the rack in the bathroom) very irritating?

What to do about it:

> Just because our feelings get hurt does not mean our children hurt our feelings on purpose, hate us, or have deep-seated psychological problems.
> When our children are challenging in public places, anyone observing us will understand that all children are challenging at times.
> If people insist on judging us, let them judge us on how we are handling the situation rather than on what our children are doing.
> Even when our children speak unkindly to us, we can forgive them and work at being the best parent we can be.

> We have a choice in how we view daily conflicts. We will feel better if we remember that these conflicts are an inevitable part of childhood.
> When children are in the middle of a tantrum, remember that it will get better if we do nothing to make it worse. Tantrums need an audience or they subside.

Over-psychologize

There are many times that insight and introspection help us figure out what is going on with our children and reveal what they need from us. But there are also times when a less-questioning approach is better. Does this blind spot affect you?

> Do you overplay your hand in parenting, perhaps by talking about an issue for too long or giving too many explanations to your children about your parenting decisions?
> Do you ask too many "why" questions, annoying your children beyond any real benefit? Do you find it difficult to keep things simple?
> Is it hard to develop an appropriate behavior plan because things seem so complicated? Are you unlikely to view behavior as just something to modify?
> Are you tempted to make excuses for your children's behavior because of your tendency to analyze?
> Do you think you have to understand what something means in order to help your children learn from their experiences?
> Do you rely too much on words? "We'll just talk about it. We'll get to the bottom of it, and then it won't happen any more. I just want him to understand the importance of this (why I need him to do his chores, why it's better if he gets his homework done before turning on the television)."

▸ Do you have your own obsessive or ruminative tendencies? Do you tend to review, rehash and rehearse too much? Is it hard to teach closure? After a conversation is over, are you tempted to circle back and bring it up again?

▸ Is your first reaction usually bigger than it needs to be: "How will they ever be able to deal with this disappointment? This will really set them back."

What to do about it:

▸ Keep things simple. Sometimes a cigar is just a cigar. Just treat the behavior. If you want something to happen less, give it a consequence. If you want something to happen more often, connect it with a reward or a privilege they already have and take for granted.

▸ Just try a few things and see what helps. It is not a big deal. Reassure yourself that many children have these problems at this age.

▸ Try ordinary discipline without any deep probing: "I'm not sure where that is coming from, but that's going to send you to bed early tonight."

▸ Avoid the why questions: It does not usually help children change faster to be asked: "Why did you do it?" "How many times did I tell you not to do it?"

▸ The true answer to the "why" question might be because they thought they could get away with it. "Frankly, Mom, I was pretty sure I would get away with it. I didn't anticipate getting caught." They are not going to tell you that, but it may be the real answer.

▸ Introspection is not the only approach. We do not always have to analyze every mistake they make. Too much psychologizing can lead to parental paralysis.

Sizing

If we see events as scarier or more upsetting, we will react one way. If we see them as predictable and manageable, we will react another way. Sizing is the only blind spot that is also a long-term goal, and the connection is obvious: *How we size moments becomes how they size moments.* They will either become resilient during times of stress by watching us deal with our stress, or they will learn that everything is a big deal and learn to fall apart.

Does this blind spot affect you?

> ➤ Do you tend to "size" things as big, even in non-parenting matters? Is it sometimes hard to view minor aggravations as minor? Without conscious effort, are you likely to respond to molehills as if they are mountains?
> ➤ Does your response sometimes make things worse rather than better? When your children are upset about a relatively small matter, are you likely to be upset as well?
> ➤ Are you more likely to turn a minor negative in parenting into a major negative, rather than turning a minor negative into a minor positive?
> ➤ When your children are hurting about a friendship, academic or athletic disappointment, do you recall similar experiences from your childhood and then tend to dwell on your painful childhood memories?
> ➤ Do you say things like "It breaks my heart to see them have to go through such difficult times?"

What to do about it:

> ➤ Remember that children will follow our emotional tone. By our response, we teach them how big something is and how much or how little power it has to hurt us.
> ➤ Reassure yourself that even though a day was a tough day,

normal childhood includes tough days. Children need occasional tough days, that is how they learn to handle them.

▸ "He is just mad at me for this moment—he does not hate me. We will get through this, we always do."

▸ "It's not the end of the world. It's just a birthday party (baseball game, etc.). Everybody misses out or messes up sooner or later."

▸ Even if we think it is huge, that does not make it huge. Sometimes we worry about things that turn out to be smaller than we thought at first.

▸ Compare what we think is big with what would certainly be big. There is a difference between children watching an inappropriate show at a friend's house and being at a house with an older sibling who has been to jail.

Project Linearly

It seems logical, but just because it seems logical does not make it correct or helpful. Many parents assume that their children's struggles at one age will still be problems when they are older. And while this is always possible, it is not typically what happens. So much of children's behavior is determined by their age. The error that many parents make is that they do not fully appreciate the developmental changes that will occur, especially between late childhood and early adolescence. Instead of automatically drawing a straight line from one point in time to another, consider that there are very few college kids in diapers.

Does this blind spot affect you?

▸ Do you add to your own stress by expecting a problem that your children have at a certain age to progress in a straight line?

> Do you torment yourself with these kinds of questions: "If this is what they're like now, what are they going to be like when they are teenagers?"
> If they take something that does not belong to them when they are young, will they end up stealing when they are older? Do you have a sense of urgency, feeling as if you have to fix this right now or else?
> Will they grow up to hate all women if they get mad at mom when they are being disciplined?
> How are they going to be able to handle high school when they are having trouble with the earlier grades in school?

What to do about it:

> Remember: Their age is a powerful determinant of their behavior. The mistakes they make at a certain age do not necessarily predict the kinds of mistakes they will make when they are older.
> Time will help, as will their cognitive and emotional development.
> It is enough to deal with the challenge of the day. The extra anxiety from worrying will not help.
> Remember that growth and maturity will occur as they move through their developmental stages. They will be more responsible and more thoughtful when they are older than they are now.

2. THE JUDGING BLIND SPOTS

Judging is almost as unavoidable as worrying. We judge their manners, organizational and listening skills, grades, and many other attitudes and characteristics as well. We compare them to other children, developmental tables, benchmarks and milestones. At certain times, this approach is somewhat helpful. How else would we know if their weight and height are appropriate or if they are reading at grade level? However, we need to be careful about the standards we are using and how our children perceive us at those times. We do not want judging to interfere with our ability to stay connected with our children and find what is possible to teach.

Invisible Rulebooks

Parents are usually puzzled at first when the conversation in therapy turns to rulebooks. The most important thing to remember about rulebooks (as the term is used here) is that they are personal and not necessarily accurate. The pediatrician's height and weight charts are based on standardized data—our personal rulebooks are not.

Think about the standards and expectations that are in your rulebook. Where did they come from? Did you intentionally invite these standards into your family life? Are they helpful? Rulebooks impose unfair judgment on our children, lead us to misunderstand their behavior, and create distance in the relationship.

It is tempting to compare our children to their peers or to a benchmark (children this age should be more compassionate, nicer to their siblings, etc.), but this does not consider the huge variation in maturity at any age. That is why we have to be careful about comparisons to peers. Our children's friends may look fine to us, but our children probably look fine to the other parents as well. The friends probably have their challenges when they are home with their parents that no one else sees. In addition, children who are not exhibiting any problem behaviors at one time may have had problems in the past or may have in the future.

Perhaps the greatest risk here is how our children come to know us. They might think we love them more when their grades are good, when their room is clean, and when they are polite and obedient. We know that our love is not conditional, but children cannot see what is in our hearts, just what we say and do. Children who mistakenly believe they are a disappointment to their parents may struggle with academic underachievement or unfortunate decisions about their weekend activities when they are older. This makes sense in somewhat of a tragic way. If they were judged when they were 6 and felt they were not a good enough 6-year-old, and then again when they were 7, 8, 9 and 10, they may come to believe that they really were not good enough for us. Instead of this being a motivator, it leaves them discouraged and at risk of giving up. It is hard to keep trying if you decide you have never been good enough for your parents and therefore will never be good enough for them or anyone else.

The flags for this blind spot are separated into two categories: the times we compare, and the times we appear as if our love is conditional.

Comparisons: Does this blind spot affect you?

> Aside from parenting, are you an inflexible person who tends to see things as black or white, right or wrong?
> Is there a tendency to rely too rigidly on guidelines that describe how "all children should be" at a certain age.
> Do you fail to consider the unique circumstances of your children's lives that influence the needs they have at any given time? Is it hard to remember the wide range of acceptable variation at each age?
> Are you stuck with the "shoulds"? Saying (or thinking): "I know how you should be at this age and you are not meeting my expectations. Your cousin does not act like this. My children should listen to me the first time I say something.

They should keep their room clean without me even having to ask. Children should not whine."

▸ Do you rely on consequences that are too big or too long-lasting in an attempt to "nip it in the bud"? Do your children try to hide their mistakes from you?

▸ Are you an impatient problem solver? Do you want to deal with a problem once, take care of it forever, and reject the idea that children repeat mistakes and change slowly?

▸ Do your children seem to believe they have to be better than they are in order to be good enough?

What to do about it:

▸ Determine the origin of the rulebooks and rewrite it until it is yours.

▸ Be careful not to confuse how they *should* be at a certain age with how *we would like them to be*.

▸ Consider what you were (really) like at their ages. Resist the tendency to only remember back as far as your late adolescent years—after you stopped being difficult.

▸ Even when they make mistakes (talk to us in an unacceptable way or bring home unacceptable grades), we can help them without making things worse by comparing them to a standard they are not presently meeting.

▸ The best comparison to make is to whom they were yesterday. Stay connected, observe and be attentive. Start where they are at, and help them move in the right direction. Work with them on what they need, rather than getting caught in the comparing.

▸ Be realistic about their academic, music or athletic potential. Do not let their childhood be filled with the feeling that no matter how hard they try they are never as good as you wish they were. Unrealistic high standards can lead to discouragement and underachievement.

> Try not to compare yourself to unrealistic standards either.

Appear As If Our Love Is Conditional: Does this blind spot affect you?

> In your attempts to help them with their responsibilities (nagging, reminding) do you come across as if you are dissatisfied with them?
> Do you allow school achievement (or athletics, or manners, or chores) to be a barrier between you and your child rather than something you use to teach what they need to learn?
> Do your children question your love or wonder if you are disappointed in them when they make mistakes? Are there times when you send messages you do not mean to send (that they are not good enough, that they have let you down again)?
> Do you say things like: "How many times am I going to have to deal with this? There is no excuse for such behavior. We've talked about this before. You know better. I asked you to do one thing, just one thing. How could you do such a thing?"
> Is your impulse (temper) control weak? Do you "race them to the basement" and allow yourself to be dragged down to their level, mirroring them at their worst?
> Are you unforgiving? Do you tend to give sermons (rant and rave, go on and on, bring up events from the past) and harbor grudges?
> Do you inadvertently teach that it is acceptable for big people to talk disrespectfully to small people? Do you permit the parent-child relationship to be used as punishment?

What to do about it:

> ▸ Be in charge of the space between you and your children.
> It is your responsibility to protect the parent-child relation-
> ship from all they do that could damage it.
> ▸ When you are thinking you have to do something to con-
> trol your child, be sure to control yourself. The heat of the
> moment may be a connection moment rather than a teach-
> able moment. If they cannot learn all that you want to teach
> them that day, try again another day.
> ▸ Know the difference between your first and second feeling
> and stay with the first feeling. Often we are sad or concerned
> before we get angry, but the first feeling passes so quickly
> that all our children see is the anger. Do not appear angry
> and controlling when really what you are feeling is concern.
> ▸ We are responsible for our emotional reaction at all times.
> Instead of mirroring them, we can use our adult voice (the
> same voice we use at work) and role model for our children
> how we want them to become.
> ▸ Our psychological presence is most important when the
> parenting moments are not unfolding the way we would
> like. Those are the times to be warm and loving and forgiv-
> ing. Handle our part of the relationship so that we will not
> make things worse or weaken them in any way.
> ▸ Remember that children sometimes wonder if their spot
> in the family is secure and whether it changes when they
> make mistakes.

Expect Payback

There can be times when our dreams and aspirations for our children
backfire. We love them and want the best for them, but that does not
mean they owe us any particular accomplishment to provide us with

bragging rights. They do not have to be the child we expect them to be or the child we thought they were going to be. They might not share our love for piano or basketball, and we want to help them become who they can become, rather than the child we envisioned.

Does this blind spot affect you?

> Do you devote yourself to your children completely, but then demand a "return on your investment" in terms of performance, academics, music or athletics?
> Do you think of your children as reflections of you and projects to be managed?
> Is it hard to settle for normal and average (instead of superior and above average)?
> Do you think your children deserve the highest grades and the most playing time on the field, ice or court?
> Does everything get personal? Do you say (or think): "How could they do this to me? I sacrifice for them, and this is the best they can do?"
> Is there a tendency to believe your children would excel if only the teacher or the coach would teach them or treat them the way they deserve?
> Are you so competitive that a school project becomes more important to you than necessary?
> Do you feel deprived of bragging rights if your children are not achieving at a superior level?
> Do you use tension between you and your children as a consequence? Could it appear to your children that you have the right to be irate if they are not meeting your expectations?
> Do you have trouble simply relaxing with your children? Can you enjoy them even when things are not perfect?

What to do about it:

> ▸ We had our turn to do the 5th-grade science projects, go to the middle school dances and be on the high school teams. Now it is their turn.
> ▸ Be careful to appreciate the children you have, rather than feeling entitled to the children you think you deserve.
> ▸ You wish them success in all things, but you cannot guarantee that for them.
> ▸ Remember: Even though we would like to be appreciated by our children, it is not always in their nature to think about us that way.

Inaccurately Insert Intent

This blind spot involves forcing an explanation on our children's behavior, as if we know why they are doing something. Instead of being connected and attentive, observing without reacting, this is more intrusive and adversarial. Children do not appreciate a parent imposing intent.

Does this blind spot affect you?

> ▸ Do you believe you know why your children act in a certain way (as if you can read their minds)? Do you tell them why they did something and remain convinced that you are right no matter what they say?
> ▸ Do you add tension to an already difficult situation by saying things like: "You did that on purpose, didn't you? I know why you did that."
> ▸ Does it seem as if their behavior is a lack of appreciation and respect when it might just be their self-centered obliviousness?

> If they forget something, do you wonder if they are just try-
ing to ruin your day or make you lose your temper?
> When they try to cover up a mistake they made or some-
thing they forgot, do you make things worse by accusing
them of lying or not caring about their future?

What to do about it:

> Remember that many problems (e.g., impulse control,
overtired) can lead to behavior that looks like disrespect.
> Children can be unaware of their parents' presence and
their words, and while this is a problem, it may not be a
problem of great magnitude.
> Some behaviors are developmentally appropriate even
though undesirable. It will not help to respond to behavior
that occurs frequently at a certain age as if it is sign of a
serious problem.
> Maybe (in their immaturity) they wrongly tried to get away
with something (lied, refused to take responsibility) and
looked like they were being disrespectful or unreasonable.
> Normal, healthy children can be self-centered and self-
absorbed. We keep things small by refusing to insert intent.

3. THE INTRUDING BLIND SPOTS

When our children are very young, we do everything for them and that is what they need. With their first step as a toddler, their first step onto a school bus as a 5-year-old and their first overnight at a friend's house, they move from complete dependency toward autonomy. Many parents find great joy in watching their children become more skilled, competent and confident. But there can be times when parents inadvertently intrude when they are trying to help.

There was one family who came to therapy because they were concerned about their 9th-grader. The boy was delightful, sweet actually. The parents were friendly, in love with each other, active volunteers in their community. There was not an obvious reason for how fragile this boy had become. He had a few good friends, his grades were fine and he enjoyed his soccer team, even made some key plays for them once in a while.

It was hard to figure out what had happened. Their lives were rich in many ways, and they had grown accustomed to things running smoothly. The mother was routinely recognized for her committee work, and the father's promotions came as expected. However, if the plumber was late or if a sister-in-law said the turkey was dry, they were upset.

His parents were devoted to him, and they hovered too much, intervened too often, and taught him that there was no such thing as a small deal:

> ▸ When he did not get invited to a birthday party in the third grade, his mother called the boy's mother to see if she could make room for one more boy.
> ▸ His father began volunteering as coach for the soccer team after fifth grade when he did not get his "fair share" of time on the field.
> ▸ In sixth grade when he was late with an assignment and the teacher gave him a "C", the parents were annoyed with

the teacher. They even went to the principal and argued that they should have been notified before the grade was given.

How were they viewing such moments? Only years later did they realize that they had weakened their son's sense of self-confidence by trying to fix every problem. At 15, their son could not deal with the predictable ups and downs of life. He had learned that he could only feel worthwhile when his life was exactly the way he wanted it to be! He had missed out on experiences that could have promoted resilience and inner strength. His parents had not seen the opportunities provided by a missing birthday party invitation, teammates who were better at soccer than he was, and an occasional late assignment, to teach important lessons.

Views Parenting as Cloning

The normal developmental process gradually leads our children towards autonomy and away from us. Parents always want this in principle, but sometimes struggle with the details. This blind spot can lead us to view our children as projects to be managed. We work with them on every school project. We sign them up for what we think they will enjoy or benefit from. When they are in high school, we tell them how many honors classes to take. This can be so intense that it triggers a "bursting into adolescence," where they react strongly against our efforts to guide them any longer.

Does this blind spot affect you?

> ➤ Do you do too many things for your children that they could do themselves? Could this weaken or irritate them? Could your actions come across as demeaning—as if you believe they need you for every little thing?
> ➤ Are you sometimes confused about where you "end" and where your children "begin?" Do you put yourself "in"

every part of their life in a suffocating way? Is it hard to respect their sovereignty? Do you find yourself mediating between your children and your spouse as if you were "in" that relationship as well?

▸ Do you come across as if you own them just because you love them? Do you think of your children as extensions of yourself, mixing up what is right for you with what is right for them?

▸ Is it hard to remember that their journey is a new and separate one, that there is already one of you and that now it is their turn to become themselves?

▸ Do you assume that how you feel about something will be how they feel about it as well? If something is important to you, do you assume it will be as important to them?

▸ Are the normal developmental milestones harder for you than they seem to be for other parents? As your children move towards adolescence, with their center shifting towards friends and away from you, and with more frequent resistance of your guidance, do you find yourself getting upset and angry more often?

What to do about it:

▸ Know that our children are separate people, loved by us but not owned by us. There is a dotted line between us, and it is important to prevent the relationship from becoming enmeshed and entangled. Show your children that you are comfortable with loving them and not owning them.

▸ Find the balance between letting go and hanging on at every age. Start early and let go gradually because they need opportunities to learn for themselves.

▸ Create two columns: One column lists the parts of their life that you control (the non-negotiable ones, worship service, off the team if grades drop), the other parts you allow them to control (hair, friends, dress, sports, and piano lessons). Review it every six months and make changes as they get older.

> Avoid hovering, micro-managing and inadvertently robbing them of important life lessons.
> Remember that children feel differently than we do, and they have different dreams and aspirations. There is already one of us, and now we allow them to pursue their own dreams.
> Even though it seems counterintuitive, some children became responsible because they had no choice (their parents were unhealthy, even dysfunctional). While this is not an argument for being an unhealthy parent, it is a reminder that children can learn from opportunities to take care of themselves.

Myth of the Smooth Road

If we could prevent our children from making mistakes or experiencing disappointments, it might not be a good thing. They might become adults who are too fragile and not competent enough. This blind spot interferes with our ability to see that children can benefit from all life events, even uncomfortable ones. If we are too shortsighted, we may prevent them from developing important skills:

> Maybe the most careful teenage drivers climbed trees when they are younger.
> There can be more to learn from a birthday party invitation that does not come than from one that does come.
> In order to be able to resist temptation, a child needs practice when the stakes are still small.

Does this blind spot affect you?

> Is there a paragraph in your job description that reads: "Tidy up all the messes in my children's lives?" Do you feel as if you have to guarantee them a smooth road in life?
> Do you try to prevent them from ever being hurt or disappointed? Does your child react to your over-protection with resentment, as if they feel insulted or infantilized?
> Have you inadvertently taught them that they can only feel good about themselves when everything is going smoothly?
> Are you interfering with their development by preventing natural consequences? Will your children end up with a lower self-esteem because they did not learn to deal with setbacks?
> As your ability to protect your children diminishes, do you react with anger at the world and all of its imperfections?

What to do about it:

> We cannot prevent them from ever being uncomfortable, even though we wish we could. Similarly, we cannot teach them to wait for the cavalry to arrive, rescue them and protect them from their circumstances.
> Accurate feedback can be growth-promoting even if it is in the form of a poor grade or getting cut from a team.
> Teach that we adjust to life as it is, that life does not unfold to meet our needs. Show them how to hurt less when life is disappointing. Use the "unsmooth" moments to teach and strengthen. What better time to model inner strength? "Of course we'll get through this. Setbacks are a normal part of life."
> Look for the advantages in the small mistakes children make at younger ages. Maybe if they are allowed to ride

their bike fast on a gravel road and end up crying, or climb a tree now and then, they will drive a car more cautiously when they are older. Maybe the organizational problems in fourth grade help them learn the skills they will need in later grades.

> Adversity strengthens and resilience grows out of difficulty. Since they are going to be confronted with such times throughout their lives, they will need all the practice they can get.

Poor Listener When Helping

It is natural to want to help our children whenever we can, but the older they get, the more our advice has to be welcomed. If we do not get the tone right, listen long enough, or convey a sense of humility about our advice, we can trigger their defenses. Parents whose advice continued to be considered during adolescence worded things in acceptable ways. They successfully fought the urge to pounce with their wisdom and directives.

Does this blind spot affect you?

> When your children are upset, do you want to help them so much that you intrude with your advice in a way that is not appreciated?
> Do they start off telling you something and end up angry with you because of your reaction? Do your children end up feeling unheard or insulted?
> Do you launch into how they should have listened to you last time when you told them something like this would happen? Do they feel blamed for not taking your previous advice?
> Is it hard for you to listen when your children are hurting? Are you so eager to tell them what to do to feel better that you interrupt or correct them?

- ▶ Is it difficult to be psychologically present for them when you want so much to tell them what they should do or should have done?
- ▶ Do you find it hard to listen long enough to permit you to see through their eyes, hear through their ears, and understand how they are viewing the moment?

What to do about it:

- ▶ Bank on our psychological presence rather than our practical wisdom. It is by listening that we teach them we will always be there for them. They can draw strength from our presence even if they are not open to our words.
- ▶ Sometimes listening is all we can do, especially at times when our children are hurting but their ears are closed. Sometimes they have to go through times that are hurtful for a while before they are able to move forward.
- ▶ Watch out for the "come here, smack" trap where they ask for help and then discount every suggestion you make. Instead, pause and ask them to clarify what it is they are looking for from you. Maybe they just want you to listen to how hard their day has been.
- ▶ Stick with what seems like nothing. Often they will hear what we say even if they are not ready to take action. Say things once and let go.
- ▶ Adults do not typically like it when they are told not to feel the way they are feeling, but if we are not careful, we say it to our children all the time.
- ▶ We want them to be open to our ideas but advice poorly given eliminates an option for them to consider. Try to make your advice sound voluntary: "All I can do is offer suggestions, I'm not sure if this will help but I remember one time . . ."

Over-helps

Prior to third or fourth grade we can probably help as much as we want, but after fourth or fifth grade, we need to pay attention to when to help and when to wait. By taking a few steps back, permitting them to go through their backpacks themselves, holding them accountable but declining to rescue, their skills develop. One mother of a 9th-grader said she was furious at the 7th- and 8th-grade teachers because they were not strong enough to prevent *her* from pressuring *them* to rescue and enable her child. Another parent said that allowing her child to miss out on a field trip because she did not get the permission slip signed was a turning point in her child's life.

Does this blind spot affect you?

> ❯ Does your love for your children lead you to a hovering and overly protective parenting style? Would you shield them from even the slightest normal childhood upset if you could?
> ❯ Is it difficult for you to allow natural consequences occur? Do you resist the idea that children can learn more from forgetting things on their own than by constant reminders from their parents? Does it upset you so much when they are making a mistake that you roar in to help, inadvertently interrupting a learning process that could have taught them something for years to come?
> ❯ Do you typically see moments as needing immediate action? Is it hard for you to see the advantages of waiting and allowing events to run their course?
> ❯ Can you justify nagging by thinking: "I just want life to be good for them. If they only listened to me and did what I told them, things would be better for them."
> ❯ Do you continue to give advice and reminders after they begin to show they do not need or appreciate them?
> ❯ Are you constantly trying to organize them or cheer them

up instead of teaching the skills to be organized and take care of themselves emotionally?

▸ Do you deprive your children of their own pride of accomplishment by helping so much that they cannot feel successful themselves?

What to do about it:

▸ If we help too much, we may wear out our welcome. Then we may not be able to help them with bigger problems in years to come.

▸ They need practice opportunities to make decisions about friendships, homework, responsibilities and time management. If we help too much, we deprive them of practice.

▸ Children can be confused about their own competence and play up their own helplessness and neediness. They benefit from always feeling connected to us but not always being rescued by us.

▸ Even though it feels uncomfortable at times, children in the long run benefit from their own mistakes more than from being rescued. We want them to feel good after *they* handle things rather than after *we* make them feel better. One way strengthens them, the other weakens them.

▸ Take some chances with the less serious issues that come up early in childhood. We can safely take a few steps back when the worst possible consequences are still small. They may miss a field trip because they did not ask us to sign the permission slip, or get benched for a game because they forgot their sneakers, but those are the experiences that teach them what to do differently in the future.

▸ It is better to be a half-step behind them rather than a half-step ahead of them. This may be the best way to allow them to assume responsibility for themselves. How can they ever remember something "all by themselves" if we are always making sure they do not forget?

➤ Some of the teenagers who struggle with grades or emotions did not learn needed skills even though they had loving and hovering parents. If someone wanted to raise a child to be dependent, irresponsible and careless they would probably nag, remind and over-help. This is the difference between teaching children how to develop a coping plan or an organizational plan they can use for years, and cheering them up so they feel better the minute they are stressed.

➤ If they think we do not have confidence in their abilities because we help so much, that message may hurt them more than the help is worth. They may resent us for treating them like a "little kid" and think we are trying to prevent them from growing up.

➤ In the long run, we want to help them have great self-esteem because they are competent and have the skills they need to master their daily challenges. Self-esteem is not something we give them by doing for them or protecting them from natural consequences.

4. THE HESITATING BLIND SPOTS

Hesitating for a few minutes while we think things through is not a problem, in fact it usually helps. However, abdicating parental responsibility is always a problem. It goes without saying that children need their parents to monitor and supervise, represent their family values, communicate and enforce rules. They need us to be walking–talking stop signs for many years. The hesitating blind spots can prevent us from seeing the need for decisiveness and ordinary discipline delivered in a calm and loving way.

Worships Their Children

Parents can be so enthralled with their children that they make too many special exceptions for them, inadvertently contributing to the children's inflated sense of their own importance. There could be a very real talent (modeling, singing, reading at an early age, art or athletics), but children do not benefit from being worshipped.

Does this blind spot affect you?

> ▸ Do you see your children as uniquely special, gifted and talented, and therefore grant them adult-like status and power?
> ▸ Have you heard yourself describe your child's artwork as amazing, singing voice as unbelievable, athletic ability as superb? Does this adoration lead you to make exceptions at home that they come to expect at school or in the community?
> ▸ Has a teacher described a behavior problem at school that you attributed to boredom or not being taught properly?
> ▸ Do you confuse parenting with friendship, needing your children to like you at all times? Does this interfere with ordinary discipline (as in, friends do not ground friends)?
> ▸ When you see a problem behavior (stubborn, rude or disrespectful), do you tend to laugh it off, viewing it as a likely strength someday when they are CEO of a big company?
> ▸ If your child tells you "their side" of a story, do you tend to

believe their version rather than what the adult (teacher, coach or principal) says? Could this lead to your children developing an unrealistically inflated sense of their own power?

› If they are busy with their sports or talent, do you ask for special favors (homework accepted late, tests administered individually)?

What to do about it:

› It can hurt children to have too much power or prestige during their early years.
› Never-ending worship from parents does not prepare children for the real world where others are also talented, and where others may or may not view them as special.
› It is best to avoid conveying an unrealistic sense of immunity to consequences.
› Children need parents who are kind and loving, and also authority figures.
› If we are reluctant to discipline because we need them to like us at all times, we may inadvertently hurt them more than we would with ordinary discipline.

Lacks Confidence in Their Parenting

Without a certain amount of confidence, parents can have trouble staying on course and using moments in a consistent manner. They might threaten and not follow through or renege on a consequence if their child looks sad or throws a tantrum. When their children demand explanations, they might feel compelled to justify their parenting decisions. And if others (in-laws, neighbors) comment about their children's behavior or their parenting, they might be extremely bothered by it.

Does this blind spot affect you?

› Have you found it hard to stick with any one approach to parenting, changing direction often, perhaps described by

others as "waffling", wishy-washy or unsure of yourself?
Is it possible that you vacillate too much and send mixed
messages to your children? Do you wish you could be more
consistent, firm and directive?

▸ Are you overly influenced by the most recent advice about
parenting (from a magazine article, television show, something you heard from a friend or neighbor)?

▸ Do you make excuses for them and explain away the need
for consequences: "I was going to pull a privilege, but since
they had such a rough day I didn't." Have you ever just
given up and stopped requiring them to do something
because it just was not worth the effort?

▸ Does the consequence sometimes seem more hurtful than
it is worth, leading you to be unsure about whether to follow through or not? Have you allowed them their weekend
privileges even after telling them you would pull them if
they did not improve at school?

▸ Do you rely on words rather than action, giving many
warnings and chances but failing to speak the language of
power: saying things once and following through on what
you say?

▸ Is it possible that you inadvertently trained your children to
ignore you by teaching them they can wear you down with
persistence? Do they ignore you because they know you
will not follow through?

What to do about it:

▸ Decide for yourself which battles to pick and which ones to
skip, but win all the battles you pick.

▸ Children need to try to sabotage new discipline approaches,
and things often get worse before they get better. Hang in
there. We need to convince them that we are going to stick
with it or else they end up with the power, and we end up
feeling powerless and discouraged.

> Reluctance to do regular discipline is not a gift to children. If you say they will be off a team if they do not get their grades up, it will be their behavior that determines whether or not they remain on the team (not you taking them off the team).
> It is better for the children to experience natural consequences and learn forever, than for us to rescue and rob them of important lessons.
> There are limits to how far we will get with words. We cannot talk to them more than they are listening so we need to consider whether they are still paying attention to us. Important issues are revisited many times over many months.
> Children (especially boys) need exit ramps or they will not take entrance ramps. That is, they are less likely to start conversations with us if the ones we start with them seem endless.
> When we know what we want to say we can almost always say it in a minute or two. Say your piece, give a consequence and move on. Start at the end of what you want to say and say it once.

Naïve

That children will try to manipulate parents is not the concern. It is only a problem if they are successful. If parents are unable to see these attempts for what they are, children can grow up with too much power, believing they have as much (or more) power than the parents. Naïve parents sometimes have teenagers who are quite stubborn, headstrong and demanding, insisting on being allowed to do whatever they want to do on weekends. They learn their parents' buttons and how to be verbally persuasive.

Does this blind spot affect you?

> Are you so trusting, gullible and easily manipulated that it is difficult for you to accept that children sometimes lie to their parents and try to confuse them or make them feel guilty in order to get something they want?

> Do you feel worn out by their response to your parenting? Can they get you to change your mind by the strength of their argument, by throwing a fit or by looking very unhappy?
> Could you be teaching your children that lines move, standards get lowered and responsibilities lightened by changing your position when they are stubborn and refuse to cooperate?
> Did you think something was cute or precious when your children were younger that was really self-centered, bossy or demanding? Were you lax at discipline, letting certain things go unaddressed that now seem like problems?
> Did your children get used to freedoms and special rights and now demand them? With your teenagers, do you accept their argument that they were "just holding it for a friend" or that "it was their friend's idea?" Is it hard for you to insist that they tell you their plans for the evening when they argue that you would not need to know if you "really trusted" them? Are you tempted to allow overnights during high school without first calling the other parents?

What to do about it:

> Be realistic about the tendency of normal, healthy children to occasionally lie or present their side of a story in a slightly distorted way so they will be seen in the most favorable light or to avoid being held accountable.
> Stall before you reply. Ask all your questions, allow them to give all their reasons. Then when you make your decision, stick with it.
> Our decision is the end of the conversation, not the beginning of the debate.
> Train them to know that you are not an easy target for their begging and whining. It is not pleasant to have an adoles-

cent throwing a temper tantrum when they do not get to go somewhere because that used to work when they were younger.

IS IT TOO LATE?

When parents first learn about these blind spots their first reaction is sometimes: "Is it too late?" They see themselves in one or several, make a light-hearted comment about there being "no rewind buttons in life," and wonder what they can do now that their children are already whatever age they are. The answer is that it is never too late. In fact, the older the children are, the easier it is to have a conversation with them about your feelings about parenting, even to acknowledge mistakes. In time, they can benefit from those conversations because they help them understand their family of origin experience better and learn about themselves by your sharing. This will be discussed again in the last chapter.

As the next three chapters describe, we are always teaching, sometimes by our discipline strategies, and sometimes by our model. If we have regrets about our worrying, judging, intruding or hesitating we can demonstrate how we learn from experience. Just as we ask them to work on their goals, we work on our goals, and we can show them by the work we do exactly how that is done.

Maybe that is what makes it perfect. Everybody makes mistakes: children make smaller mistakes, and adults make bigger mistakes. People change and grow, and their mistakes point them toward their needed work. Our children are always working on being the best "them" they can be, and we are always working on being the best "us" we can be. They learn about forgiveness from how we treat them and ourselves at the times of mistakes, and they learn how to forgive themselves and us by our model.

Chapter 5

Honoring Sovereignty

Understanding our blind spots helps us see our children's mistakes and disappointments so we can help them develop. We pay attention to and try to resist the worrying, judging, intruding and hesitating. With practice, our ability to be in the moment with our children improves, and we observe more often without reacting. Without blind spots, we see our children's individuality, strengths and weaknesses more clearly, and focus our efforts on accepting them exactly as they are at all times. Mistakes and disappointments are considered teaching opportunities rather than catalysts for anger or anxiety. By remembering they are being the best child they can be even when their behavior is stressful, we honor their sovereignty and show our acceptance, even when they need to be disciplined.

Many parents hurry over this idea and just give it lip service:

> ➤ "Of course I accept my children. It's just that they are rude to me, and that's not acceptable."
> ➤ "Nobody loves their children more than I love mine, but you can't expect me to put up with these kinds of grades."
> ➤ "Don't tell me it's just a mistake. They've been acting this way for months."
> ➤ "I'll forgive them, but first they have to apologize."

And countless other examples.

Honoring our children's sovereignty means we are comfortable with their uniqueness. They are always who they are. Sometimes they are warm and loving and cooperate with us fully. Other times their behavior challenges us. They might act like a younger child or they might act like an older child. Either way can be stressful. In fact, they might act exactly the way they are supposed to act at their age and that can be stressful, too! But none of it has to be viewed as so stressful that it prevents us from responding to them in a supportive and gentle way.

By working on our priorities of parenting, we make sure that we are always able to breathe in and breathe out calmly, to view their behavior as acceptable at all times, even when they are informing us by their behavior that work is needed. They are different from their siblings, from the neighborhood children, from our nieces and nephews, and from their classmates, and this is exactly as it should be.

We know when we are honoring their sovereignty

- ➤ We are next to them (not angry or impatient) when they make mistakes.
- ➤ We are next to them (not weakening them) when they are disappointed.
- ➤ We are teaching rather than fixing.
- ➤ We understand that the pace of change is slow.
- ➤ We are being the best "us" we can be.
- ➤ We view them as being the best "them" they can be.

We know when we are not honoring their sovereignty

- ➤ We are unrealistic about their academic, interpersonal or athletic ability.
- ➤ We want them to be better than they are "right this minute."
- ➤ We are not considering their temperament, life circumstances, how they have been parented to date, or the stress in their lives.
- ➤ We are dissatisfied with how they are acting and try to force them to change faster than they can (push the river).

INDIVIDUAL DIFFERENCES

Parents may resist the notion that their children are "perfectly acceptable" even when _____. How each parent completes this sentence sheds additional light on the subtle influence of their blind spots.

Even when:

> They are rude and disrespectful.
> Their grades are poor, and they do not even seem to care.
> The phone never rings. They never get invited for a play date or a birthday party.
> They fight with their sister and brother whenever we are not looking.
> They repeat the same mistake for several months.

Darlene was trying to be comfortable with this idea of individual differences as it pertained to her 8-year-old daughter, Hannah. She and her husband, Phil, had been married for ten years before they learned they were going to have Hannah, and were both thrilled because it had taken so long to become pregnant. Hannah was their only child and they were both devoted to her completely.

As Darlene worked on honoring sovereignty with Hannah at times of mistakes, she realized she was quite good at it when it was just the two of them at home. But it changed when Phil was home or whenever they were with relatives. She talked about feeling embarrassed when Hannah misbehaved, as if her husband, parents or sisters were judging her parenting. And she knew she was not making this up because she had been part of such conversations with her mother and sisters over the years when the judging was about other parents.

She talked with Phil directly and this helped. She considered sharing her feelings with the others, but she did not believe that would help. It bothered her that she was parenting in a harsher and more critical manner at those times. Ultimately, she decided that the others should not judge in the first place, but if they insisted, they should at least be realistic about how 8-year-olds behave, especially when they are away from home, tired, or overly excited. And, it would make more sense if they judged her on how she handled the challenging situation rather than judging her based on what Hannah was doing.

Darlene had to address the feeling of embarrassment in order to be able to honor Hannah's sovereignty, but once she did, she developed a discipline plan, and Hannah's behavior gradually improved during the visits to the relatives. It also helped that she became more accepting of Hannah at the time of the mistake.

Other parents have to address other barriers. Many of us want our children to do very well academically or athletically, and may resist the possibility that they are not gifted or talented. What about the average children? What does this approach look like with children who play a sport but do not excel, or do an average amount of homework and bring home average grades? At times, there might be an advantage to having a child evaluated to rule out a learning disorder or an attention problem. And sometimes extra practice, tutoring or additional training opportunities helps. But that is not the main issue here. Some children still hit limits after the tutoring and the additional help. What then?

The intruding blind spots can interfere with a parent's ability to accept limits. By intruding, some parents may inadvertently send the message to their children that they are not good enough exactly the way they are. It is just as important to honor our children's sovereignty when they experience disappointments as it is when they make mistakes. Maybe they will play on a junior varsity team instead of varsity. Maybe they will go to a two-year college instead of a four-year college. It would be unfortunate if our inability to accept them as they are led them to struggle with self-acceptance in later years.

Parents who struggle with the hesitating blind spots can feel uncertain about what to do because they are not sure they completely understand what their child's behavior means. But what if we are "just" supposed to *start where they are at*, stay connected to them and help them any way we can? If we think about it in this way, parenting strategies emerge. Do we want them to do something less or more? Can we teach resilience or emotional calibration?

STARTING WHERE THEY ARE AT

Instead of comparing them to how we think they should be, we start where they are at and help them as best we can. We work at staying connected with them at all times, (including when the mistakes are repeated and the pace of change is slow) and resist the worrying and intruding. Viewing them as "perfectly acceptable" at all times does not prevent us from talking to them about the problems, disciplining them and teaching them our values; but it permits us to do all this while we teach them to view themselves in a positive light.

Perhaps the most obvious implication is to parent each child differently. Even if they are the same age (multiple births or adoptions), they are unique individuals with their own histories and circumstances, needing whatever they need from us at the time. All of our children will make different mistakes and experience different disappointments, and they will develop at their own pace. Tell your children at the earliest possible age that in your family "fair is not equal." After a few months of whining, they will get used to the idea that you do not compare them to each other, and they are not to compare how one is parented with how the other is parented.

Children come with their own abilities and interests. Some love to read so much they would rather not go out to recess or sign up for sports. Others live for dance or basketball. But children can also struggle with reading and be awkward or clumsy. Are children with lower abilities supposed to be crushed by life? These children need parents to protect them from school, report cards and the assumption that sports are an essential part of childhood. Honoring sovereignty helps us teach them how to be comfortable with their own abilities and prevents us from hurting them with unrealistic expectations or demands.

Many children love to play with other children, but not all children. Some would rather be home, entertain themselves, have time alone in their rooms, or just be with their parents and siblings. Maybe they are introverts (perfectly normal) who need peace and quiet to recharge their batteries. If they are not lonely or hurting about a lack of friends, there is probably no action needed. If they wish they had more friends, we can work with them to develop the skills needed to make friends. But extroverted parents of introverted children often assume the presence of a problem where there is none, and add unnecessary tension to the family by their concerns.

Parents often bring their strong-willed children to therapy with complaints about endless power struggles about chores, manners and an assortment of issues pertaining to cooperation. Honoring a strong-willed child's uniqueness requires a parent with great calmness and the ability to see past the day's power struggle. It takes two people to have a power struggle, but only one person to prevent it.

The toys need to be put away, and there is no cooperation in sight. The parent can offer a choice: "You may cooperate and put your toys away before the timer goes off or not. If not, I'll do it, and you'll lose a privilege." No power struggle. We do not have to get them to put the toys away (that is the trap). We just have to follow through with our discipline plan. If we are not able to honor the way they seem to be wired, we can have years of daily battles and too much distance and stress in the parent-child relationship as a result.

Some children have a harder time understanding the sequence of events than others. For example, a parent can nicely ask a child to take out the garbage, and the child could say, "in a minute." A few minutes later, the parent might ask again with a slightly more impatient voice. After being ignored several more times, the parent might react in anger. Some children genuinely seem to think the sequence began with the parent's head exploding! They remember what the parent did, but not what they had been doing just before.

We want to help them understand the true sequence of events, but we will not be able to do that if we react with impatience or anger.

That will only flip the focus to our behavior. In fact, the better we do our part of the relationship, the more likely it is that they will be able to look in their own mirror and see how their behavior was not appropriate and needs to change.

Parents also worry about the friends their children select, and some children do seem to be attracted to a certain kind of adventurous, risk-taking friend that might be a reason for concern. The strategies are clearer when there is obvious danger: We always intervene when there is a health or safety issue. But it is not always clear when the other children are mostly harmless, just occasionally inappropriate. This example is included here, because if we stay connected with our children (and focus less on the other children), we might sense what our children see in the other friends. Whatever is drawing them to the adventurous friends is inside our children, and that is where our energies need to be directed. By talking with our children about how they view this friend, we can set the stage for future conversations about friendships and help them with their friendship choices for years to come. If we try to pick their friends for them, they might tell us less about their friendships in the future. We will talk about this again in Chapter Seven when we talk about protecting the connection.

We want to parent so they keep sharing and valuing our guidance. It is the only way we will be able to help them when they are teenagers. Prior to adolescence, children can sense when their sovereignty is honored, and it is a powerful strategy that calls them to us. And it is never more helpful than at times when our children are challenging.

One mother sent me a copy of a note she gave her 11-year-old daughter after a heated argument:

"I'm sorry I lost my temper and yelled at you. If I had it to
do over differently, I would have stayed calmer and pulled
a privilege because of the way you were talking to me. I will
work on that. Now that I'm calmer, I want you to know that
it is always an honor to be part of your journey and that

mothers and daughters can fight sometimes even though they love each other a lot. I love you more than you can know— even when you talk disrespectfully to me and even when I lose my temper. You have to make mistakes at times, and a lot of kids your age make this mistake from time to time. You have the right to make your mistakes, and that doesn't give me the right to make my mistakes. I'm going to work hard to allow you to be you—even when that includes mistakes, and I'm going to work hard to be calmer at all times."

She did not get a note back, but she did get a hug and an apology.

BEING PREPARED FOR ADOLESCENCE

James and Cheryl were worried about their second of four children when they started therapy. They were happily married for twenty-four years. Cheryl had been home with the children at first, returning to her career as a social worker when their youngest started school. James was the employee assistance counselor for a national department store. Both were level-headed and soft-spoken as well as being experienced with adolescent development.

Their oldest, Cindy, sailed through high school and was enjoying her first year of college, living on campus a few hours from home. Kent was a sophomore in high school, and they were worried about him because his attitude toward school was poor, and he was sullen and withdrawn. The first few meetings were primarily "finger-pointing" meetings: Kent described his parents as favoring his perfect older sister, and James and Cheryl pointed to Kent's disrespect and lack of effort.

As Kent came to believe that his parents only wanted him to achieve for his own ultimate benefit, good college choices and job opportunities, rather than wanting him to be like his sister, he gradually improved. James and Cheryl returned to therapy with their younger children off and on over the years. Towards the end, they talked about how hard parenting had been "even for them" and how teenagers should "come with a manual." Their thoughts led to several conversations about what such a manual might include.

James had enjoyed the traffic story and came up with one of his own for the beginning of the manual. He had been driving on a hilly, two-lane country road about an hour south of the Twin Cities (Minnesota) on a tough winter-driving day. It had been snowing all morning, the road was slippery, and he was driving well under the posted speed limit. The drivers behind him were encouraging him to drive faster by tailgating. Suddenly he came to the top of a small hill, and there were cars everywhere. A truck had skidded into the ditch, and the next two cars lost control when they swerved to miss him. There was just enough road open for James (and the tailgaters) to navigate between the truck and the two cars.

When he got home and told Cheryl about his close call, he added that it reminded him of parenting teenagers! He explained that chaos can occur without warning when you are driving on snow and when you are parenting teenagers. The end result in both cases depends on what you were doing before the chaos began. That reminded Cheryl of an orienteering class she took years before in preparation for a camping trip in the Boundary Waters Canoe Area of Northern Minnesota. While her instructor was teaching her how to use a map and a compass, the emphasis was on *staying found* rather than what to do once you are lost. *Staying found* with our children might be similar to handling moments prior to 11, 12 and 13 with 16, 17 and 18 in mind.

Since normal adolescence (even at its best) challenges our ability to honor sovereignty, the accurate information presented below can help navigate through the transition to adolescence.

Some parts of adolescence start early:

> ➤ It is not helpful for us to be surprised by the inevitable. Even 5th-graders can be self-absorbed, self-centered, demanding and obnoxious: as if the sun rises in the morning especially

to warm their face. It is possible they will have little concept for us as real people with our own lives and our own feelings.

> It is important to start having talks about dating, sex and relationships years before they need the information to take advantage of their ears still being open.

> Anticipate their center shifting with friends becoming more important. They may not allow us to help them as much as we want to. They will only view us as "all wise, all knowing and cool" for so long.

> Be careful about continuing to parent them as if they are younger than their actual age.

Sooner or later most parents will wonder:

> "Why do I have to repeat myself?"

> "Can't they see that I only want the best for them?"

> "Why can't they be like I was when I was their age?"

> "How could they complain about being bored when they haven't even done what they need to do?"

> "How could they spend an hour resisting a ten-minute chore?"

> "Will they ever figure out how to stay organized?"

Hardest to hold when they need us the most:

> When insecure they appear obnoxious, with little insight. They may not see their own behavior but perceive our reaction to them as more disappointed or angry than we actually are.

> At times, the obnoxious behavior is a facade to cover their inadequacy. They are in the middle of a constant self-evaluation process, with others appearing better than they are (taller, cuter, thinner, smarter, and more talented).

> When they are faced with feelings of inadequacy, they might appear arrogant. They can be insecure and image-conscious—almost paranoid at times about where they fit in and whether or not they belong.
> When they need guidance, they reject help. Their search for autonomy interferes with their openness to our advice. They push us away because that is the work they have to do. It is hard for us when we want to help them but it helps to remember that they will not be teenagers forever, and we want them to be completely autonomous as young adults.

Identity hopping:

> Be careful not to panic when they are "trying on" different identities. The identities are often in reaction to our values (as in "I don't believe in God anymore"). It is as if they are screaming, "You don't own me," and "I'm not your little baby."
> Presentation of self becomes important and a potential area of conflict. They will be preoccupied with appearance issues (grooming or not grooming on purpose).
> Rapid, confusing changes occur for them and for us as we try to stay connected. We are never completely sure who they are going to be from day to day. Their planning abilities and judgment are poor. They are emotionally volatile and act without thinking.

Deep and shallow:

> They are between childhood and adulthood, alternating between deep and shallow. They can be very caring and sensitive about the poor, the environment, and natural disasters, and at the same time frivolously demand expensive things and want the furnace turned up while walking around the house wearing very little.

- ▸ At times they are filled with a sincere and deep faith, asking questions such as: "Why can't people just get along?" or "Why does there have to be war and misery?" At other times they whine and complain about attending worship service.
- ▸ They seem uninterested in spending time with us when they are busy but resent us if we can not drop everything when they are not busy.
- ▸ They love and miss their grandparents whom they rarely see, yet argue about visiting them if their friends, whom they see every day, are available.

Viewing relationships:

- ▸ There is a tug of war between parents (and all that parents represent—family values, safety, future) and friends (fun, excitement, adventure).
- ▸ They cooperate better with a parent who makes time for them and a teacher who likes them. It is important to feel valued. "Am I being treated fairly?" "Am I being listened to and heard?" They are willing to accept a bad grade or a consequence to "punish" the teacher or parent.
- ▸ Their perceptual weaknesses may lead them to see us as loving them more when they achieve or use good manners than when they do not. They are vulnerable to misunderstanding our efforts to guide them and help them grow and develop. There will be power struggles over small matters.
- ▸ It is difficult for them to reach out to their younger siblings. They are often not ready to be a good role model.
- ▸ They tend not to appreciate how lucky they are, how much they have (good schools and health care), and they throw a fit if they cannot get the latest toy or gadget.
- ▸ They throw themselves into intense pseudo-mature relation-

ships with peers before their communication and conflict resolution skills have sufficiently developed.

SHIFTING STRATEGIES

The above observations can help you be realistic about adolescence and the importance of shifting of our parenting strategies. James and Cheryl's oldest (Cindy) was never a concern to them academically or socially, but Cheryl remembers how surprised she was when, at 12 or 13, it was no longer enough for her just to be right about something. She also had to pick her words carefully. Before, Cheryl could simply tell Cindy what to do and how to do it, and give her advice, welcomed or not. Now that approach led to tension. When we are familiar with the predictable changes of adolescence, we are better able to honor their sovereignty by shifting our strategies from *power to influence*.

This might be evident in small ways:

› More attention devoted to picking and skipping battles.
› Thoughtfully deciding what parts of their lives we can safely turn over to them and where we need to retain control.
› Being realistic about how they view us. Did we feel grateful for everything our parents did for us when we were 14? Did we care if our parents liked our boyfriend or girlfriend when we were in high school? Did we ever lie to our parents to avoid a consequence or to be able to do something we really wanted to do?

And it might require deep work on our part as well. They are dressing differently, thinking about boys and girls differently. Dating and parties are on the horizon. It is clearer to us now more than ever, that we want them to feel comfortable talking to us about their real lives. Not the sanitized version most parents get. The best strategy for increasing our influence is to convince them in hundreds of ways that we honor their sovereignty and that we "get it." They are separate people from us and we do not own them. We talk about choices a lot. If they choose not to cooperate, they will get a consequence, and that is all they will get. They will not get a sermon, and they will not have to deal with our anger.

When they need our advice, we want their ears to be open to our words: That is why it is more complicated than being right. We listen to them as long as we possibly can and stall as long as possible before we respond. Then we might preface our remarks:

> ▸ "That's a tough situation you have there. I'm not sure what to tell you."
> ▸ "You're a smart kid, you'll figure it out."
> ▸ "Have you thought about it this way?"
> ▸ "If this were my decision to make, here's how I would think about it."
> ▸ "Here's my opinion, but you might have your own opinion."

Our excitement about their journey away from us is emphasized. Mostly we want them moving towards health, and we would like to be invited along for the ride. We say these words at first and we might get blank stares back. The message sinks in gradually over the years. They will not respond like this: "Oh, I get it, you are the best parent, and now I will share everything with you."

They may hardly be listening to us in the first place! But if we start early enough and if we present ourselves in this way consistently, they will come to know us as kind, forgiving and approachable parents.

INSTANTANEOUS FORGIVENESS

Perhaps the greatest benefit of honoring sovereignty is that it makes it easier for us to forgive our children in the instant between their action and our response. It sounds simple, but it is not. One parent had a minor traffic accident on her way to a therapy session and said she knew she had a problem when she found herself using a more forgiving voice to the driver who crashed into her than the voice she used with her daughter the night before.

Bob had such a hard time with forgiveness that his wife, Joan, "dragged him to therapy" (his words). He worked days as an electrician, and her nursing job required rotating shifts. They did not bring their two boys, 7 and 10, even though Joan was worried about how Bob handled the evenings, homework, chores, bath and bedtime routines.

Bob did not see anything wrong with yelling at the boys when they "needed to be yelled at," and he thought they were trying to manipulate Joan by pretending to have trouble falling asleep and crying when she got home. Joan was worried that the boys were genuinely hurt by what Bob said and how he sounded.

He had been raised by well-meaning parents who yelled and had quick tempers. Instead of learning to discipline children with a forgiving tone, Bob learned to yell. He knew that Joan agreed with him about the importance of teaching the boys to be responsible, so they agreed to a discipline plan with very clear expectations and consequences, and he agreed to use a softer voice.

In a later session, Bob told me that three things made the difference:

> He knew that he and Joan shared the same goals.
> He did not want his sons to be scared of him. He remembered very clearly what that felt like and the distance in his relationship with his parents.
> He wanted the boys to be in trouble when they did not do what they were supposed to do, rather than being in trouble himself!

The last comment was accompanied by a grin but there was wisdom in it as well. He started saying things like, "I hope you can get your chores done before 7:00 so you'll be able to have a friend over tomorrow," and "That's too bad, now you won't be able to use the computer tomorrow because you missed your bedtime."

He learned to respond to his sons with a forgiving tone without backing off on his demands. Even though there were still times when they were given consequences and lost privileges for not cooperating in a timely manner, it was not long before they were asleep before Joan got home from work.

HONORING SOVEREIGNTY HELPS WITH DISCIPLINE PLANS

As we will see in the next chapter, the best discipline plans include words like these that refer to sovereignty:

> ▸ "I don't own you, and it is a privilege to be part of your journey."
> ▸ "You will have to make these decisions for yourself, but I will always be here to guide you and offer advice if you will let me."
> ▸ "You are not a puppet and I am not the puppeteer."
> ▸ "I have rules at home that you have to deal with. If you don't follow them, you get into trouble, but I can't crawl inside of you and make your hands move."
> ▸ "I can't make you be a successful student."
> ▸ "I can't make you empty the dishwasher. All that I can do is say, if the dishwasher is not emptied by 7:00, I will empty it and pull a privilege."

Chapter 6

Disciplining with Reassurance

Discipline is an important part of teaching the long-term goals. However, many parents confuse discipline and punishment and the difference is more than just word selection. Parents are in charge of themselves when they are disciplining, and they are not when they are punishing. The two are different in fact and tone, and the difference is immediately obvious to children. When parents are in charge of themselves, children can look at their own actions and take responsibility for themselves. When parents punish in an angry or heavy-handed way, children are more likely to focus on the parent. Discipline for growth feels a certain way; the anger and revenge of punishment feels differently.

The goal is unambiguous: comfort them, support them, *and* make them pay a price for their mistake. Connect their behavior with privileges or consequences, tell them how they should handle themselves the next time, then (take a deep breath and) make them dinner. The privileges can be things they take for granted like television, having friends over, and being driven places. The consequences can be small, short and symbolic, with the tone loving and forgiving.

HOLDING CHILDREN ACCOUNTABLE

We want to avoid hurting our children when we discipline, but this approach does not lead to an abdication of parenting. We need to hold our children accountable for their mistakes. It is important for children to be told when their behavior is unacceptable and how they need to change. Pulling privileges and giving consequences are the tools we use, and these do not have to include interpersonal tension. By paying close attention to the times we discipline calmly and the times we slip into a more punishing approach, we learn where our need areas are.

First, do no harm. This is the parent equivalent of the physician's Hippocratic Oath. Do not make things worse by your parenting. When you are dealing with one problem, do not handle it so you end up with two problems. Children are more likely to remember what we do long after they forget what they did in the first place.

When we use a respectful voice and hold them accountable, they stay connected to us *and* their behavior improves. There is forgiveness, not anger. Instead of, "How many times are you going to mess up until you finally get it right," we say, "How may I help you with this?" Rather than being judgmental and critical, we are accepting and peaceful. We forgive them because they are ours and because we understand that they are children. Children make mistakes, and we remind ourselves that the pace of change is never fast enough. We treat them better than they are treating us, and we discipline in a reassuring way by saying: "We'll get through this together. This is why children have parents. This is something that's hard for you now."

One father asked: "Aren't we supposed to be their parents, not their friends?" He was worried that appearing calm and forgiving would lead them to think they could get away with anything. He was not sure it would be enough to give them a consequence without including a harsh tone or a raised voice so that they would know that he was serious.

It *is* enough. Children have more potential than dogs, and dog trainers have been modifying behavior for years! We can have confidence that if we show up, stay true to our values and do nothing to make things worse, things will get better. For example:

> ➤ "With these kinds of grades, you can't play soccer (watch a show, use the computer)."
> ➤ "I won't be able to drive you to soccer practice because you haven't been doing your chores."

Then, with the plan in place, you wait. "It wouldn't be right for you to have friends over this weekend when you are behind in your assignments." The hard part is not what words to use, it is being able to say it calmly and stick to the plan without any harsh words or tension.

The alternative is to punish them *with our relationship.* Some children get confused about whether or not we love them when we are angry. We know that they are loved all the time, but is it obvious to them when they are being disciplined?

There are long-range implications of confusing discipline and punishment. One mother said she remembers that it was hard to please her parents when she was growing up because their range of acceptable behavior was narrow. She grew up believing there were only two choices when her behavior did not fall within their narrow range: She was either a bad child (a disappointment to her parents), or her parents were mean and unreasonable.

This dilemma is not shocking. Children who struggle during their adolescent years frequently decide it was not their parents who were being unreasonable, they *really were bad kids.* Disciplining with reassurance addresses the behavior problem without unnecessary parent-child tension. We are not gentle and forgiving to protect their self-esteem or to prevent them from feeling bad. We are gentle and forgiving because we are adults, and we know we can modify their behavior without appearing disappointed or critical.

Holding them accountable and forgiving them are not mutually exclusive. Children learn more from decisive action (a password preventing computer use, no friends over, extra chores, or removal of electronic games) than they do from an angry sermon. Warnings, threats and nagging are not typically effective. Too many words can escalate a situation.

Children need to realize that we have so much power we do not even have to raise our voice or repeat ourselves. It is good for them to see decisive power, and to see it delivered calmly and briefly. They will have fewer behavior problems and will be less manipulative. It is the opposite strategy, using a lot of words, too much explaining, and too much emotional baggage that leads to whining and begging. One mother needed to listen to her music with headphones to highlight both to herself and to her children that a conversation was over when she said it was over. They began to realize that Mom really did have power: "She's not even listening any more—she's got her headphones on."

I remember working with one parent on a standard behavior management plan for her 9-year-old son who was not taking care of his responsibilities. After a few weeks she told me that while her son was still struggling with his behavior, *her* behavior had noticeably improved! Now that she had a plan, she was calmer and more able to avoid the interpersonal strain that had been invading their relationship. His chores did not always get done, and he still lost privileges at times, but the tension between them was gone. She said that what helped was the confidence that the plan in place would help her son change as soon as he could change. And she was working hard at staying realistic about the pace of change.

WHEN THEY SPEAK DISRESPECTFULLY

Many of us would never have dreamed of speaking to our parents the way our children sometimes speak to us, perhaps because of the threat of physical discipline. Since then, hitting and spanking has been eliminated as a "recommended parenting strategy" because we know the emotional scars are too deep and long-lasting. It is not healthy to grow up being hit by someone twice your size, especially someone who is supposed to be looking out for your well-being. Even though we might be able to stop the "backtalk" faster with hitting or spanking, we choose not to parent harshly. Non-physical consequences will decrease the rude and disrespectful comments in time, just not always as fast as we would like. Our patience with their pace of change prevents us from hurting them emotionally at times when they need to be disciplined.

EXPLAINING OUR DECISIONS TO CHILDREN

Parents may lack confidence that a consequence and a brief talk is enough. They may be tempted to continue a conversation after it should end. Conversations should almost always end when children say: "But why?" or "How come?" or "It's not fair." They rarely want a serious explanation. They are all little attorneys and just want the conversation to continue! They do not want us to leave the table. If we stop speaking, it is over and they have to accept that we are not going to change our minds.

However, if you think they are genuinely interested in the reason for your decision, it will not hurt to explain once. More often, the child's request is manipulative. Maybe we will change our mind if they keep pressuring us. This is particularly true when they learn that we do change our minds sometimes. It is better to stall before we make our decision, permit them to say their piece, and then teach them that once we make our decision, the conversation is over. By the time your children are teenagers, it will help if they know you are a parent who does not change a decision once it is made. Remember, the people we explain things to at work are usually the people who supervise us. We do not want to confuse our children so they come to believe they have power over us and deserve an explanation whenever they demand one.

My wife and I had something on our refrigerator when our kids were little about separating the child from the child's behavior. It helps to think about their behavior problems as coming from some genuine place such as their age, their stress, or something unknown. Our children will drive us crazy in fairly predictable ways at each age, but when we are their allies rather than their adversaries, they will change and grow and stay connected to us. In this way, when they are older and they begin to think about how they were raised, they will have every reason to feel fortunate.

DISCIPLINE AND KNOWING WHAT TO TEACH

At first you might have trouble finding what to teach, but here are two reasonable starting points:

> ▸ Mistakes at every age can be viewed as connection-strengthening opportunities.
> ▸ Disappointments at every age can be viewed as resilience-strengthening opportunities.

Our love for our children does not rise or fall based on whether they have made a mistake or not, and their worth as a person is not hinged on every achievement and accomplishment. When mistakes and disappointments are handled with discipline and reassurance, they become useful and exciting moments. But if our blind spots interfere, the mistakes lead to hurt feelings and tension. For this reason, it is not "what they do" at each age that predicts their future; it is "what we do next." It helps to parent with a long-term view.

Preschool

Parents of 4- and 5-year-olds frequently describe cooperation problems. The children refuse to do what we ask. They may even run away from us at a neighbor's house or at the park. *Parents of older teenagers know exactly how they wish they had responded when their kids were younger.* But what becomes obvious in hindsight is not always easy to see in the moment. All 4- and 5-year-olds are going to act this way from time to time, some more often than others. We choose to view these moments as opportunities to begin the lifelong work of separating a person's basic worth from their mistakes and flaws.

By our words and our calm emotional presence, we show them

that they are loved and valued at all times even when they are running away from us. There is no emotional distance created by our actions. They just cannot go back to the park for a few days because of the mistake they made. The discipline is not the tricky part, forgiving instantly and protecting the connection is. There is nothing easy about staying calm and confident when they look at us and say something like: "I won't do it, and you can't make me."

Our children's journey from preschool to high school will be filled with mistakes. Even if we cannot do very much to *prevent their mistakes,* at least we can teach them about us and how we *view their mistakes.* In our minds, we always see them as *perfectly loveable,* it is just that "darn old mistake" that we have to address. This will be important at all ages.

Preschool children get too tired, too stimulated and resist transitions. We might say things like, "This is not your finest moment," or, "How would you handle this if you had it to do over again?" Think about the 4-year-old boy who has a meltdown when it is time to leave his friend's house. That might be a perfect time for teaching him that he will not always get what he wants. We do not have to prevent the meltdown. Rather, we can say to ourselves that as long as we make sure he does not benefit from meltdowns, they will gradually become less and less frequent. We say the obvious words: "Honey, I know you're frustrated, but we still have to go." Later, when his ears are working again, we can add something like, "You were frustrated because you wanted to stay at your friend's house, but now that we're home, you're feeling better."

A mother was caring for her 3-year-old in a restaurant. The child was throwing a tantrum—screaming and sobbing—but the mother was gentle and soothing, unexcited and comforting. In just a few minutes, her child had quieted down. It was apparent that her young child's behavior was not aggravating her. Rather it "called her" to be relaxed and confident. This came naturally to her, and she did it well. She understood that her child was too tired, too stimulated (or "too" something). She was not angry or embarrassed. She accepted and honored her child's predicament.

When they are little, it is usually obvious that their problem is due to some stress, and we forgive them before we react even when we do not fully understand what the stress is. A meltdown in a public place might be upsetting if we thought our child was being impossible on purpose or if we worried that we were being judged by the people around us. But most of us are able to think about the young child's meltdown in a way that leads to feeling calm rather than tense.

It becomes harder for us to be able to handle older children's challenges similarly. They have meltdowns, too! Many of us become less skilled at calmly comforting the 11- or 12-year-old because by then the meltdown does not call us to be comforting. Now, their meltdown elicits a power struggle.

Thoughts precede feelings, and both precede actions. We will be calmer if we *expect* them to be who they are. Instead of needing them to be appropriate at all times, we can work at expecting them to have all kinds of days, even though that will include some undesirable behavior. We observe without reacting immediately, choose how to view the moment and make a decision about disciplining with reassurance.

Marie was a 2nd-grade teacher and a mother of three girls (7, 9, and 12). As is true for most teachers, Marie understood how her 2nd-grade students' behaviors were influenced by their age. But she was not at all ready for her 12-year-old's behavior! Nothing her younger girls did led Marie to respond in an unkind way. This had also been true with her oldest until the last month or two. Now, when the 12-year-old acted self-centered, stubborn, or arrogant, Marie's abilities to "protect the connection" were nowhere to be found. Even though she was a teacher, she needed to become familiar with what being 12 did to an otherwise delightful child. With accurate information about this developmental stage, Marie became calmer and more successful at presenting herself to her oldest in the loving way she had always used with her younger children.

We help our children with their problems by viewing them as "acceptable" even when they are not little angels. It starts with our ability to *view "what is" as acceptable* even when stressful and requiring parental intervention.

One parent was having a hard time with this idea. "How can it be acceptable when my son has eight assignments missing?" She decided to make an effort to be light-hearted, respectful of her children but humorous instead of tense. After a few weeks, she came up with these classic one-liners:

> ➤ "I love you, you're good enough, your computer has a password on it."
> ➤ "Let me show you how acceptable you are while I take you off the team so you will have more time to spend on some important things."
> ➤ "I will not drive you to soccer the way you're talking to me, my perfectly acceptable sweetheart."
> ➤ "Sorry, honey. Even though I'm crazy about you and all that, I just wouldn't feel right about letting you have a friend over this weekend with such a messy room."

Just as the mother in the restaurant had been able to be close to her young child, we need to be able to be close to our older children. Even when they have meltdowns, use time poorly, leave chores undone, or push us away; they need us to be comforting. Sometimes it is only with hindsight that we see that our children were hardest to hold when they needed us the most. We do not lower the standards for their behavior or make excuses for them. They need to learn to avoid meltdowns, talk to us respectfully, tell the truth, do their chores, and be kind to their siblings. And we want to keep them closely connected to us while we teach these lessons.

Kindergarten—Second Grade

Six- and 7-year-olds often have trouble listening the first time they are told something. And they do not always do what they are supposed to do without reminders. It is essential that they see us as kind and benevolent but also as *a force to be considered*. With our quiet voice and a gentle look in our eyes, we want them to know that their privileges come from us, and if we have to repeat ourselves, they can be lost. They will not lose our love, and they will not be treated disrespectfully. We will not raise our voice, we will not have to. Instead we might say:

> ▸ "You'll get your privileges back as soon as you cooperate with me better."
> ▸ "Everybody is working on something, this is what you need to work on."
> ▸ Then, you could wrap it up with your sweetest: "Dinner in five minutes, honey."

Third—Fifth Grade

Sooner or later, most 9- and 10-year-olds will leave something important at school or forget about an assignment until the last minute. We can show up, stay true to our values and address the problem. They are the ones in fourth grade, and they will either do their homework or they will not. They get the grades they get. We develop a discipline plan that connects their performance with privileges and consequences. That usually is not the hard part.

Remember: Do nothing to make things worse. Be careful about providing too much help. While it seems like good parenting to communicate with the teacher daily and wrestle with children and homework nightly, those strategies actually interfere with important lessons and create unnecessary stress and strain.

When they get the grades *we know* they can get, they will have more fun, better privileges, and opportunities to join teams and clubs. However, we do not appear more loving when they bring home great grades, and less loving when they bring home disappointing grades.

This can be hard to see in fourth and fifth grade but easy to see by the time they are in high school. Children need to learn how to work their way through their disappointments and discouraging times. We want them to sense our confidence in them, and that is why we allow them to deal with certain struggles themselves. We know it is only by struggling and succeeding themselves that they become capable and resilient.

Sixth—Eighth Grade

Even though we understand the physical and emotional changes 11- and 12-year-olds are experiencing, it is still upsetting to hear them speak immaturely about each other's developing bodies. There is not any controversy about whether it is wrong when they do this. As always, we say our piece: "That's not acceptable. We don't talk about people's bodies in that way." Perhaps after a warning or two, we add a symbolic consequence. Maybe they have to write a two-page report for us on disrespect, exploitation or how the media uses bodies to sell products. But we try not to look angry.

Parenting includes dealing with mistakes that are hard to celebrate. However, it is better to discipline with reassurance, and prevent unnecessary distance between us.

High School

While it is hard to see when they are young, our children will become interested in dating and going to parties. And chances are they will continue to make mistakes and experience disappointments.

How can we help them if their first relationship does not seem to be a healthy one? What if our child or the friend is too clingy? What if one is controlling or possessive? We often know what they "should" do. After all, we have so much more life experiences than they have. It makes perfect sense that we would have wisdom to share.

Will their ears be open to us at that time so we can help them with those challenges? Did we handle the moments prior to high school so that this will be likely? If so, they will be more open to sharing with us. That will give us a chance to teach what it might mean if a 16-year-old boy thinks he owns his girlfriend. Or about the advantages of double dates, group dates and dating several people, but not one exclusively. We will know what we want to say. Whether they will listen is harder to predict.

This is where "disciplining with reassurance" connects with "honoring sovereignty." Since age is such a powerful determinant of children's behavior, we try to use whatever they present us with to teach the long-term goals. Different ages provide us with different opportunities. Just as 14 is "famous" for striving for autonomy and pushing parents back, 6-7- and 8-year-olds are famous for forgetfulness, emotional sensitivity, separation problems, nightmares and a reluctance to try new things. Nine- and 10-year-olds want to have exclusive rights to a best friend and are often clingy and possessive. If they do not have a best friend, 9- and 10-year-olds can be upset and think they are not likeable.

Parenting always takes the age into account. Many challenges of childhood will improve with the passage of time if we do nothing to make them worse. Six-year-olds will not make 6-year-old mistakes when they are ten. Two-year-olds will not be in diapers when they are in college. Most of us are peaceful about their time in diapers because we know it is normal. We view the years in diapers in a way that keeps us calm.

Often it seems as if the problem is either "the age" *or* "something serious." But something could be partly due to the age and partly a sign of something serious. For example, 9-year-olds can be thin-skinned, sensitive and easily hurt. Many will grow stronger with time, but not all. For some, these characteristics will linger and may even lead to feelings of depression in years to come. The best strategy is to honor our children and their sovereignty as unique individuals, making whatever mistakes they make, growing at their own pace, and experiencing their disappointments. Even though there are guidelines, there really is not an exact way every child should be at a certain age.

We use the best information we have to understand our children and their behavior. And while there are helpful standards we can use to judge their height and weight, it is more complicated with children's emotional and developmental issues. One girl told me she had been quite hurt by her father's expectations, thinking she was not good enough for him. He was crushed to hear that, since he had only been trying to help her be the best she could be. He thought he knew how she should be at each age, but in trying to help her, he inadvertently hurt her deeply.

When we remember that we have choices in how to view our children's behavior and circumstances, we are better able to stay patient and forgiving. But we still take action! They need our help if the problem is due to their age or if it is not. One parent summarized her comfort with this approach by saying: "Of course they need our help, they are our children. We allow them to be who they are, and we help them without judging."

Nothing will influence whether our teenagers continue to allow us to help them more than how we disciplined them when they were younger. The tone of voice and the look in our eye is enormously important. One father was helped by imagining a camera, always nearby, always on, recording him (only him) whenever he was disciplining. It did not pick up sound or sight of his children. His goal was to be able to handle himself no matter what his children were doing so he could watch the recording later without regret.

We cannot let their mistakes and our reactions to their mistakes become our relationship. By using consequences rather than intense emotions, we help them grow as fast as they possibly can without falling into the trap of starting with one problem and ending with two. It is not the consequence that makes them think we are angry or disappointed with them, it is the tone. All children, even preschoolers can become comfortable with the idea that parents give consequences when mistakes are made. But it is important to save the intense voice for safety issues that could someday take them away from us.

Jeff and Karen brought their 17-year-old son, Alex, to therapy with very real concerns about grades, friends, driving, and curfew violations on weekends. They knew enough to wonder if he was making other unhealthy decisions when he was away from home that they had not heard about yet. It took several months and hard work on all three of their parts to get things back on track. One thing Jeff and Karen would have done differently is they would have used a less intense approach with important but not critical issues prior to adolescence, saving the urgent tone for potentially life-altering ones. Alex was tired of hearing their warnings and reprimands years before they even started talking to him about alcohol and parties, dating and driving.

Their mistake is easy to understand. They did not want him learning bad words on the bus, watching inappropriate shows, or wearing jewelry and insignias that were disrespectful. If they had been able to talk to Alex about these kinds of concerns differently he might have been able to hear and take seriously their concerns in later years. Karen would get worried and sound pushy and frantic. Jeff would sound angry. Neither was able to stay with their first feeling of concern. Children do a better job of staying closely connected with concerned parents than they do pushy, frantic and angry ones.

Jeff and Karen stayed in therapy after Alex was better. It was not only the voice they used when they were worried, they were too intense in many aspects of family life. They said they wanted to do things differently with their two younger children. The following discipline plan was developed for them and for other bright, committed parents, who have trouble balancing the need to guide their children, encourage change, and treat them better than they deserve while disciplining.

DISCIPLINE PLANS

> ▸ Remember that just as songs have music and lyrics, discipline has words and tone. It helps to have "pretty good" words and "pretty good" consequences, but the tone is everything. There are many choices as to what words and consequences to use, but the tone must be kind, forgiving and reassuring.
>
> ▸ Trust that they will accept the consequence if the tone is

not degrading and the interpersonal tension is kept out of the situation.

> Accept that moments requiring discipline can escalate rapidly. It is as if they are a smoldering fire, and we want to be the sand or the wet blanket that keeps it small or puts it out, not the fuel or kindling that makes it bigger. We want to use thinking words rather than fighting words.

> The choice of consequence is not a search for the "right" consequence—we can pick whatever we think will help. We do not have to pull anything we do not want to pull. The search for the right consequence can be a sign of our impatience.

> Consequences can be small and short because they are primarily symbols of our displeasure. The behavior will not necessarily change faster with bigger or longer-lasting consequences.

> No doubling (or tripling) the consequence just because the mistake repeats itself. This is called: "you know the drill," since the consequence can be pretty much the same for repeat offenses. Children know what to expect, and this helps. If the child does not seem to be taking you seriously, that might be a reason to change the consequence to one that has more impact. It does not necessarily have to be bigger or longer-lasting, just different.

> All consequences can be divided into two categories: Those requiring the child's cooperation and those not requiring cooperation. Sending a child to their room requires cooperation. Deciding not to drive them anywhere for a week does not. Certain children resist cooperating with our consequences, and if we pick one that requires cooperation, we may feel powerless, and our children may react to our discipline in a way that escalates matters further.

> We can insist that something is done "right away" or not. Some children dig in their heels. At those times, we can

give them a choice: Either they do it right now or they do not. One way they do not get a consequence, the other way they do. We can even do what we asked them to do—as long as we give them a consequence later for not cooperating.

> If we say we are going to take them off a team if they do not improve their school work, we have to follow through. If they do not improve, *we* are not letting their teammates down by taking them off the team. *They* are responsible for their lack of progress and for losing the privilege of being on the team.

> Rely on your discipline plan. Trust that, in time, children respond to privileges and consequences.

> Expect progress to be slow. Better to wait one, two or three months for change than to hurt children unnecessarily. This can be the difference between saying, "This can't go on," versus, "I'll be there for you as long as it takes."

> Be careful about hopping from one strategy to another. If you try too many different approaches, it might mean you are not sticking with any one long enough. This may encourage your children to try to sabotage your efforts.

> Give children one reminder only, and then act. Do not nag.

> One minute is your limit for giving advice and sermons. They are not usually listening after that anyway.

> There are always choices and options. If children get into trouble at school, and it has already been adequately dealt with by the time you hear about it, maybe it can be considered over. If you are not sure that your child took it seriously, you can add something at home.

> Privileges can be anything children already have and take for granted. All we have to do to turn those things into privileges is connect them with a desired behavior. "From now on, in order for you to _____ (have a friend over,

watch a show, use the computer) you need to have this done first." We do not have to get them to do what we are asking, we just have to follow through on our discipline plan.

> Doing one of our chores, working with us in the garage or the yard, writing an apology or an essay, drawing a picture about what they did wrong, or doing volunteer work with us, are all reasonable consequences.

> Charts are helpful because then you do not have to think fast. Instead of feeling pressure to come up with a consequence each and every time something happens, you can put a checkmark or a red dot on a chart and review it once a day.

WHEN THEY "JUST DON'T CARE"

Jeff (more than Karen) had very clear memories about getting angry when Alex would resist his discipline. At times, Alex would sound cooperative, as if he was just about ready to do whatever it was Jeff wanted him to do, and then do nothing. But what was really hard for Jeff was when Alex would respond to a consequence with an "I don't care" attitude, baiting him to escalate.

Children have different temperaments and react to discipline in different ways. None of them are likely to say: "Thanks for disciplining me, and by the way, that was a perfect consequence." Fortunately, we do not need them to care. We just need to be at our best when they are not at their best. We do not escalate, and we do not double the consequence. We remind ourselves that the pace of change is never as fast as we would like.

What if they have a similar attitude about school? When the stakes are as high as they are with homework, tests and grades, it is difficult to be patient. But if our discipline plan does more harm than good, the problem could last longer than otherwise.

What could be more important than school? There is no question that children need to do their homework, study for tests, and plan ahead for projects. How do we address this and conserve parenting resources at the same time? School performance is not a battle that can be skipped.

Children question the importance of education at predictable ages, typically when they are in fifth, sixth or seventh grade. We see them using their time poorly, "forgetting" an assignment, maybe even lying to us. This is a perfect time for taking them off a team or not allowing friends over on the weekend. But we do not scare them with frightening images of their own future. We do not say: "How are you ever going to succeed in high school if you can't even take care of sixth grade!"

If parents get upset about a grade, they run the risk of sending the message that the child is a disappointment to the parents. That is a bigger deal than the low grade. "I'm not good enough for my mother." We do not want our children to believe they are not worthwhile just because they are making poor choices about the importance of school or time management, or if they have not yet developed sufficient organizational skills.

It is better to be their reservoir of confidence, saying, "We'll get through this together." We hold onto the longer time frame, not just the next report card. We use the moment as it is, with their underachieving, lack of motivation, and disorganization, to teach our children about us, our values, and what happens to children in our family who do not take school seriously. They continue to be loved and treated well, but they do not have very much fun.

Children whose parents act like this become stronger and more ready for the future. How could there be any other outcome? At the moment they are falling behind in school, they hear something like:

> "I'm not mad at you, but you are off the team until you get your grades back up. Kids your age sometimes have a hard time with this. We'll work on your time management and your organizational skills. That's what parents do."

Privileges help you get more of the desirable behavior, and consequences help you decrease the unwanted behavior. Think about the difference between:

> ➤ "Now I get to help you with this. This is what families are for. This is hard for you. We'll probably be talking about this a lot for now."

And

> ➤ "This will not go on. How many times am I going to have to deal with this nonsense?"

Both discipline approaches address the behavior, but they play out quite differently over the years. Why do so many parents find this difficult? Because we are supposed to be able to pull this off while we are making dinner, doing laundry, staying caught up with work and volunteer commitments and taking care of our ill or aging parents. It is plain to see why it is hard, but that does not change its importance.

PARENTAL DISAGREEMENT

Not only do our children need us to learn about viewing moments and our blind spots, but in families with two parents, there is the additional need for parental agreement. It is not surprising that this is difficult.

Who knows why we fall in love and how we decide whom to marry? The only certainty is that this decision does not consider who will partner well with us as we parent! It is more the norm than the exception that people who love each other and who both love their children will have trouble developing a unified parenting strategy. At best, this leads to lengthy conversations between spouses about how each one is viewing what is going on with the children. At worst, it leads to a blame game and marital problems.

Since children need a common approach from both parents, it is important to work together to develop one. Ideally, two parents will be able to talk in private about their parenting strategies. When something unexpected comes up, as it certainly will, the first parent on the scene rules. That is, the second parent supports the first parent in front of the children. Later, they can review it and decide together how to handle similar situations in the future. Here are a few potential areas of conflict between spouses about parenting:

PITFALLS

> Two strong-willed parents both accustomed to being right may believe their way is the only right way.
> One parent looks at the other's parenting with disrespect and somehow communicates this to the children.
> One parent may have more power in the marital relationship than the other. If this person is with the children more, the other parent can be marginalized. If the person with more power spends less time with the children, this can only lead to significant relationship problems.
> Intense disagreement can lead to indecisiveness in parenting that can hurt the children.
> Couples with communication problems in general will have problems coming to agreement in parenting, but the problem may not have much to do with the children and their behavior. Sometimes marital work is needed first in order to be able to address the parenting issues.

THE STEPPARENT ROLE

Much has been written about divorce, blended families and the stepparent role. One observation that is worth a mention here is that children may not welcome a stepparent into the family and because of this, discipline can be tricky. If the children refuse to accept discipline from the stepparent, it can be helpful to keep discipline in the birth-parent's job description, at least at first and at times permanently. The stepparent can be more like a warm and loving godparent, or favorite aunt or uncle. This strategy, where the stepparent takes on more of a supportive, nurturing role and less the role of the disciplinarian seems important and accommodating. At times, this can be the difference between a successful "blending" experience and one that is upsetting for all family members.

Disciplining with reassurance will help children change their behavior at least as effectively as disciplining with anger or impatience. And the possible damage to the parent-child connection is never worth the risk of an angry or impatient tone. Our focus now turns to protecting this connection.

Chapter 7

Protecting the Connection

While it may sound insignificant, there is very little in parenting more urgent than "protecting the connection." *It is the most critical parenting task.* It may strike us as obvious, but when parents are not able to protect the connection, children are hurt. The dilemma is accomplishing this at all times, regardless of what our children are doing. It helps to have great compassion for the hard work of childhood and consider that they are being the best child they can be each day. If our blind spots get in our way, we may act in a way that injects too much distance into the relationship with our children.

Parents often say it helps to remember that much of the stress of family life stems from children acting their age even when they are making their mistakes. After a particularly rough day, one mother said:

> "I am exhausted! He's been making 8-year-old mistakes all day. And a year from now, he'll be making 9-year-old mistakes. Is there no end to the joys of parenting?"

Her light-hearted perspective was possible because she had accurate information about how age influences behavior. When we are home alone with our children, and they are difficult, we work to stay calm, and when others see our children being difficult, we work to not feel embarrassed in any way. Trust that reasonable observers will be impressed by your parenting during difficult times rather than shocked by your child's behavior.

Our priorities help as well. It helps if we are not organizing our parenting around impossible goals: keeping them happy at all times, preventing mistakes, or if we cannot prevent them then eliminate the mistakes as fast as possible. We do not want the parent-child relationship *to become* the accumulation of stressful moments poorly handled. It is better for them to feel our support and reassurance even when they need guidance or discipline.

Accepting the normal chaos of family life allows us to focus our resources on the most important issues. Some parents ask their children to clean their room on Saturday mornings, instead of every day. Others resist intervening at times of sibling rivalry as much as possible. And viewing the ordinary disappointments of childhood as inevitable, even strengthening, helps as well. If we try to do too much, we run the risk of becoming exhausted.

The "blank week" exercise is useful. Start with a blank piece of paper, perhaps as summer is winding down. Make a grid with the days of the week across the top of the pages and morning, afternoon, evening in the rows. Write in the most important activities that promote your family's wellness and stop when the week is full. While it may be hard to believe, many families start with the least important activities and then do not have time for their children's most important needs. It is better to do one or two less "enrichment" opportunities than to have frantic weeks.

The goal is for our children to know we are crazy about them *the way they are not the way they could be.* It is simple to picture but very hard to pull off.

> ➤ "You are perfect even with this mistake."
> ➤ "I love you just as much when you make mistakes as when you don't make mistakes."
> ➤ "You are the best "you" you can be. That's why we don't compare you to anyone or anything else."

With disappointments, the goal is for them to believe that they are good enough for their parents, even though math is hard, their team lost because of them, or grades do not come easily.

Life happens, and children do whatever they do. We are supposed to make it all meaningful. After all, when we think about all the long-term goals, we actually need all kinds of teaching opportunities, including the stressful ones. And just as we are compassionate about the hard work our children have to do, we are forgiving of our own humanity and the times when this "obvious" goal eludes us.

PARENT-CHILD BOND

Many of us learned about the importance of connecting and staying connected with our children when they were infants. This bond *increases* in importance over time. What do infants do that could threaten the connection? Even if they have trouble sleeping or cry all day, we usually stay gentle and loving with them. It is obvious to us that when they seem to be pushing us away, they need us to be close. As our children move from infancy through adolescence, this should not change. When they are pushing us away they need us the most.

This next story comes from a graduate level course I teach. The students are within a year of obtaining their doctorate in psychology. When this topic came up, one student said she thought bonding was only important during infancy. Nothing could be further from the truth! In fact, staying connected with our children is never easier than when they are infants.

All we have to do is think about how they change and how they push us away as they get older. While parents agree that infants are not difficult on purpose, it becomes less apparent with 8- 10- and 12-year-olds. Their provocations seem more intentionally obnoxious, and in some cases they are. At those times, our goal is to not be provoked.

It reminds me of a father who called me on a Monday morning with a lighthearted observation he made after attending worship service the day before. The sermon had been on patience, and he had enjoyed it thoroughly. On his way home he realized he was trying to get in front of another congregant so he could get out of the parking lot sooner. Enjoying a sermon on patience does not make us patient, it is a goal that requires deliberate effort. Similarly, acknowledging that "protecting the connection" is a worthwhile goal, is not the end of the discussion. When a parent commits to protect the connection, the work has only just begun.

Our children do not see what is in our hearts, they can only see the look on our face and hear the words that come out of our mouths. That is why their perception of us is always different from our perception of ourselves. We are constantly introducing ourselves to them, many times each day. Imagine them flipping a switch and seeing approachable, avoidable, approachable, avoidable, as we parent. They accumulate thousands of images of us, and they tend to remember our actions more than how they challenged us. Even if they are perfectly obnoxious, and we are patient, patient, patient, and then our head explodes; six months later, they remember our head exploding and not our patience.

WHERE IS THE DANGER?

Of all the reasons parents start therapy, "connection" is one of the least often cited. Friendship and achievement issues, moodiness and sibling problems, chores and backtalk are more likely. In fact, some time is usually needed before parents can see these moments as "connection-strengthening" opportunities. Handled well, children grow closer to us and more confident; handled poorly, the problems linger and may even worsen.

How we parent every day changes when we understand that the long-term danger pertains to the connection. *Disciplining with reassurance* will change our children's behavior without needless tension. *Honoring sovereignty* prevents us from judging and comparing them to arbitrary standards. The difference on any given day is subtle, the long-term results quite dramatic. Our children feel our support during the times of their mistakes and disappointments and continue to share. There will be no reason for them not to. And when they are older and bigger mistakes and disappointments happen, we will be able to guide them and rejuvenate them because they still allow us to be close.

THEIR DEVELOPING AUTONOMY

We always took the diaper bag on outings when our children were very little, and a similar approach is needed throughout childhood and adolescence. Whatever their need, we had what we needed in the bag. Similarly, we need to be prepared to take care of them at every age. If only it stayed as easy as remembering to bring crackers, wipes and an extra set of clothes!

Now we need to bring our viewing skills, not only on outings, but wherever we are every minute of every day. One father said he gave himself this little pep talk each morning:

"Bring it on kids, poppa can handle it. The worse the better. Let me show you what I'm made of. No matter what you throw at me, I'm ready for it. The more times you mess up, the more I can show you how much I love you. The more you know how much I love you, the better it will be for both of us."

You probably have your own pep talk. As long as we have our viewing skills, we can be at our best and protect the connection from their worst moments. When we are dealing with a problem, at the very least we can prevent it from escalating into a second and third problem. Let them be the only one throwing a fit. If nothing else, we can avoid adding fuel to the fire. The following statements, coming from a parent, typically add nothing except fuel:

> ➤ "How many times do I have to tell you . . . ?"
> ➤ "There you go again."

> ➤ "If you had only listened to me."
> ➤ "If you had done it the way I told you to."
> ➤ "If you had followed my advice."

It helps to think of the emotional space between us as if it were physical space: close is desired, too much distance is not. *We are in charge of the space.* They cannot be. Our psychological presence can be brought to all the moments of parenting with long-term benefit. Here is another driving story to help clarify this point.

Kelly was a new teenage driver. The road was winding and narrow with a speed limit of 20 miles per hour. She was probably going the speed limit but did not see the boat and trailer coming at her until it was too late. She swerved and hit a fire hydrant. Only the car was injured. Her friend said: "Your dad is going to be furious." While they were still shook up from the impact, she said: "He won't even be mad." That is the goal, no interpersonal distance created or added by our actions. One parent used a rubber band analogy: Children pull and stretch and add tension but if we are nimble and responsive we keep the tension manageable.

Even parents who understand the necessary autonomy work of late childhood are not always successful at viewing the behavior in a peaceful enough way to stay at their best. For example, it is not uncommon to hear complaints about 10- and 11-year-old children who are self-centered, disorganized and irresponsible. What is not common is to hear a true acknowledgement of how the striving for autonomy looks on a day-to-day basis at these ages:

> ➤ This is a time of rapid and confusing changes for children.
> ➤ They need to push us away as part of their journey towards autonomy.
> ➤ They do not have their act together yet and resent our reminders at the same time.
> ➤ They are starting to flex their muscles a bit, test the limits and push us away.
> ➤ Emotions are strong, impulse control is weak.

What if we could view these early acts of defiance as more beneficial than nerve-wracking? The stakes are still relatively small, their whereabouts are known 100 percent of the time and the worst that could happen is not very scary yet. Maybe they are learning words we would rather they not learn, watching shows we would rather they not watch, telling immature jokes, not using their full potential, etc. They begin to see a diminished role for us in their lives yet they are completely dependent on us for years to come. They dig in their heels, refuse to apologize, and act as if we are invisible or worthless. Honoring this part of their journey means we follow our discipline plan, breathe in and breathe out, forgive them and reassure them that even with this, they will be fine.

These are the years when our behavior will determine whether they are still connected to us as teenagers. Even if they will be talking to us less and spending more time alone in their rooms, we can help them continue to see us as kind and loving parents who are always there for them. And the most powerful time to convince them of this is when they are doing their autonomy work.

I AM NOT YOU

While a generalization, the main dynamic at work as adolescence approaches seems to be their declaration: "I am not you." What you get from your child depends on how you have been acting towards them. Parents with the most rules, especially if those rules are perceived as petty, probably get the most defiance. If you micromanaged their homework and their backpack, they may underachieve. Did you pick their friends for them the last year or two? Maybe part of their autonomy work will be proving to you that they can do it. As 12 becomes 13, they are not actually charting their own course in life, just making sure that you are not charting it either. Instead of genuinely finding themselves, they may just be pushing you away.

Sometimes they are so determined to show us they do not need us anymore that they refuse to fill us in on how things are going. "How was your day?" "Fine." This exchange is not a great predictor of how the next five or six years are going to go.

If they come home and something is obviously bothering them, you are not able to simply follow them to their room and help them as in years past. It is complicated by their changes. In fact, one mother said she hated that all the rules of parenting were changing, and that the rules were being changed by her children! At these ages, children cannot even remember to ask us to sign a permission slip for a field trip, and we have to *follow them* into adolescence! After twenty-five years working with families, the irony is hard to miss.

During this time, they may want to work through something on their own to show us and themselves that they do not need our help. But often, they still need our help more than they want to admit. The instinct to hug them, kiss them and sit right next to them until they feel better is still there. However, it just may not be welcomed.

Instead of imposing ourselves on them, we can let them know what we notice, "You seem upset today." And then if their reaction, "leave me alone," is not inviting you in right then, let them know your ears are always open. You can respond with a statement like: "You're in charge of when and if you share, and whenever you feel like talking, I will feel like listening."

And when they choose not to share when we know they need us? We stand back, because it is almost always best to prove to them that we understand that sharing is up to them, and is not something we can control. We try to handle it so they circle back after a while, (sometimes measured in months or years rather than days or weeks) voluntarily seeking out our guidance. Once they do, we will be glad we allowed them the dignity of struggling some on their own.

One part of the irony is that we have to appear comfortable with a decreased role in their life in order to retain a significant role. Before our children reach adolescence, we convince them of our love and devotion to them by being there for them and doing for them. Then, the parent role shifts, and we have to show them how excited we are about their developing autonomy. The children who feel this permission do not seem to push their parents away quite so forcibly. We do not fear them becoming their own person. By honoring the work they have to do, we become more likely to be invited along for the part of their journey when they need us the most.

WHERE TO FOCUS

Because of the autonomy work, we have to keep our focus between our child and us, rather than between our child and their world. While there are certain exceptions (e.g., abuse, harassment, bullying) when some dramatic intervention is necessary (calling the police, a school administrator or the school bus company), it is typically better to use our children's life experiences to teach them how to deal with such experiences in the future. For example, if our children are in dance or hockey and the dance instructor calls them fat, or the hockey coach speaks disrespectfully, we can help our children decide whether they want to continue in those activities, rather than trying to get the dance instructor or the coach to change.

It is tempting at times to try to change the world so our children will not be uncomfortable, but that strategy runs the risk of sending the message that the world is only there for their comfort. We are surrounded by an imperfect world, but at least we can teach our children about the power they do have to protect their boundaries from unwelcome comments. And children benefit from understanding the difference between what they can control and what they cannot. One day a teacher may scold them in front of the other students, or an adult at lunch, recess or on a scouting weekend accuses them of something unfairly. These are unfortunate experiences but perfect for teaching that how they feel does not have to be determined by what happened. These are the moments that permit us to teach about resilience and emotional calibration. We will not be able to see it in this way if we are focusing beyond our children.

If we blame the friend when they watch an inappropriate show at the friend's house, we miss the chance to hold our children accountable for their actions. And even though we wish there was less "garbage" out there (television, radio, magazines, billboards, movies, and the Internet), we know we will be able to help them more over the years if they come to us and tell us what they saw and heard.

In fact, keeping our focus on our children and their relationship with us provides a plan and a sense of direction. Our children's connection with us is like a safety net or a buffer protecting them from all that is out there. Since we will not be completely successful at filtering out all the inappropriate elements of childhood, we need a plan for when they are exposed to something undesirable. By viewing the inappropriate show as an antibody, a weakened disease germ, similar to the vaccinations our children receive, we know how to proceed. With our guidance, they learn how to view the event. Like an immunization process, we protect them from being harmed in the future by how we use what they experience as children.

EXTERNAL LOCUS OF CONTROL

The above incidents share one key characteristic: They are perfect for promoting an internal locus of control. We model that the dance instructor's comment or the coach's communication style does not control how we feel. There is always a choice in how we view an event. We resist the perspective, summarized by the phrase "isn't it awful," that insists that we feel terrible whenever anything imperfect happens. Instead of getting overly upset by a teacher's action, we point out ways our children can grow by focusing on what they did that led to the teacher's remark.

At one extreme, there are parents who teach the opposite by making excuses:

> ▸ "That teacher didn't know how to control his classroom."
> ▸ "If only the coach didn't favor those other players."
> ▸ "All the women on my side of the family are like this."
> ▸ "You made me lose my temper."
> ▸ "He (the child) started it, he wears me out. I can't stand another minute of his behavior."
> ▸ "He was so disrespectful to me that I yelled at him."

> ➤ "This is the way I've always been and I can't change."
> ➤ "Everything was fine until those kids moved in next door."
> ➤ "You're just like your father."

It is not usually the life experiences that automatically hurt our children. Life just happens, and it is our reaction that either strengthens or weakens children. How we view life's inevitable ups and downs determines what we teach our children when they experience something unpleasant. Just as we show them that their behavior does not cause our response, we also teach that their response to what happens to them can be modified by how they choose to view it.

FRIENDSHIP PROBLEMS

Perhaps nothing sends children home crying in third, fourth and fifth grade more than friendship problems. At those times, it is tempting to focus beyond our child, blame the other children for acting in an unkind way and inadvertently miss a powerful teaching opportunity. Picture this routine lunchroom scene. One child is carrying a tray of food and walking towards an empty chair next to a classmate. As he approaches, the seated child says he is saving the seat for a friend, and the child with the tray walks on.

This scene could be viewed in different ways. The seated child could have been more sensitive. The walking child could have simply found another seat. How you see this might depend on which child was your child! The seated child probably did not mean any great harm to the walking child, he just wanted to spend lunch with a friend. However, if the walking child came home crying to *you* about this scene, perhaps adding: "Nobody likes me and I'll never have any friends," you can see how tempting it is to focus beyond the child, and fail to see this as the opportunity it is to address long-term goals.

Be careful about interviewing for pain: "Did anyone leave you out today?" Instead, explain that on some days the seat gets saved for you and some days it does not. And some days you save the seat for your friend and maybe discourage another child from sitting next to you! It is childhood, and our role is to teach them how to view it so they are strengthened and not weakened by everyday moments.

They will have times when they have all the friends they need and times when they do not. During those times when they have friends, other children will be going home crying for other reasons. And what could possibly be a better opportunity to teach that they do not need unkind friends? Maybe it is the friendship problems before adolescence that allow us to teach them not to be clingy, needy, or desperate to belong when they are older.

TIMES OF DISAPPOINTMENTS

Other disappointments will occur. Recess can be a lonely time, talent shows have limits to the number of participants, and sports can be frustrating. When we focus on our child and teach what the moment allows us to teach, instead of trying to change recess, talent shows and sports, our children become stronger. Do they need to learn skills on how to join in at recess time? Perhaps not making the talent show is a chance to talk about not getting everything we want. One parent felt comfortable speaking very plainly about this to her 10-year-old:

- ▶ "The other children sing better than you do. Dinner is in five minutes."
- ▶ "There will always be people smarter, better, richer, prettier and that's why we don't compare. We're comfortable in our own skin and in our own lives."

Disappointments provide many important teaching opportunities. Mistakes do too.

CHOICE OF FRIENDS

What if the problem is not being excluded, but our children seeking out friends who concern us? It is not uncommon for 6th- and 7th-graders, as part of their identity hopping, to see what it feels like to have friends their parents would not select. The knee-jerk reaction is typically to prevent the friendship from existing. And there are times (health and safety issues) when that is the best response. However, when the friend is slightly negative, but not dangerous, we probably want to handle it with the goal to keep our children talking to us about friendships for years to come.

After all, it is our child who is doing the selecting. If we interfere with one friend but do not address their desires for such a friend, they may keep looking. To be able to influence the decisions our children make about friendship, we need access to their thoughts and feelings, and we need their ears to be open when we speak. We may end up with more influence over their friendship selections when they are older by taking a few deep breaths and a few chances with certain friends when they are younger. Since it is basically a tug of war anyway, with the peers tugging from one direction, we want to have solid footing to keep our children connected to us. We are not likely to be as exciting as the friends, and the autonomy work is tilting against us as well. That is why we have to do all the ordinary parenting work, especially the discipline, in a way that protects the connection.

PUSHING US AWAY

One father said he had the information about autonomy stored away in a part of his brain where it was not always available when needed. Many of us fail to observe without reacting when our 10- 11- or 12-year-olds are rude, tell us they hate us, and engage in needless power struggles. Later, when we recall that they were "just acting their age," we can apologize if our actions weakened rather than protected the connection. However, it is better to develop a way to store the information so it can be retrieved faster. This is where our viewing skills and our insight into our blind spots becomes very important. Their behavior—no matter how obnoxious and disrespectful—does not have to make us react in any certain way.

PROTECTING BY STALLING

Stalling at first sounds similar to the hesitating blind spots, but there is a significant difference. Where the hesitating blind spots (worships the child, lacks confidence, naïve) interferes with knowing how to parent, stalling helps us know how we want to parent. Where the former leads to a lack of effective discipline, the latter can prevent an immediate and regretted action from us. Some parents get into the habit of responding to younger children without pausing, perhaps stemming from concerns about safety (stove or bathtub). But if the choice is between parenting poorly or parenting better with stalling, then it is a gift to our older children for us to learn how to stall.

See if you can decrease the pressure you put on yourself to respond immediately. Is it coming from an unrealistic expectation you have for yourself? One parent said she thought "good parents" could always think on their feet, and come up with just the right thing to say at all times. Nothing could be more unrealistic. *Good parents stall.* Give yourself a chance to think things through, talk to your spouse or a friend, tell your children you will get back to them as soon as you can. Do no harm. Stay with your first feeling (concerned rather than angry). They can often wait a few minutes or a few hours for your response. Try saying: "If I try to deal with you right now, I might not handle myself well. Maybe later, after I calm down, we can talk about this again."

USE FEWER WORDS

In business there is a point of diminishing returns, when additional money poured into a business does not increase its profitability. This applies to the number of words used in some family conversations. If you want to protect the connection, then do not repeat yourself fifteen times until things deteriorate. Since our children usually stop listening after a minute or so, it is almost always better to say what you have to say in the first minute and move on. After you are done, try not to swing back an hour later and say the one thing you did not think of saying before, or do not think they fully understood.

There is one situation that calls for as many words as our children will allow. In between the challenging times (when they are not in trouble), we can initiate conversations that will enthrall and fascinate them. The topic is human sexuality and all that it entails. Here, timing is everything, and the optimal time is years before they need the information.

Since we want our children to learn about human sexuality from us, we have to be early. And 3rd- 4th- or 5th-graders will almost always sit and listen (wide-eyed) to us when we talk about the facts of life. They will bombard us with questions that will lead to opportunities to give them important information about dating and relationships, power imbalances and control issues. Even though the information is not useful or relevant to them yet, the intimate sharing sets the stage for future talks. They come to know us as approachable parents on this most important topic.

The same conversations with 6th- and 7th-graders usually do not go smoothly. They are more self-conscious and often reluctant to ask questions for fear of being embarrassed.

ACTING OUT AND TASK MAINTENANCE

While there are many reasons for children acting out, a frequent scenario involves their need for attention from parents. It does not make it acceptable, and it is not an excuse, but it directs us to a strategy.

Susan, who was an anthropologist and taught at a local college, was the mother of two children (7 and 10). Her husband worked in a technical field for a software company. They were as busy as any family and the hectic pace of life contributed to watching the clock a lot, hurrying to get somewhere and last minute crunches for school projects. Susan talked a great deal about tasks and task maintenance.

She was struck by how much of her relationship with her children was devoted to taking care of things or making sure they were paying attention to important projects and deadlines. Her children did not do well when too much of their time with Mom and Dad was spent on homework, driving to an activity, reminders about chores and getting ready for bed. There was a need for a minimum amount of the relationship to be reserved for "anything but" tasks. She said it did not even matter what they did (read books, watched movies, walked or rode bikes), as long as it was anything but tasks.

She also believed that families had become so busy that there was a risk of thinking that taking care of the tasks was the most important part of parenting. Her children were harder to handle (whining, complaining, fighting with each other) when they did not get their minimum of "anything but" time. Even though it is hard to resist getting swept away, it is important that we not move so fast that we miss moments.

LOVING OUR CHILDREN IS NOT ENOUGH

How we are perceived by our children matters more than what is in our heart. One teenager said she did not feel comfortable telling her parents about how a friend was pressuring her to do something because, "They never think I can do anything right anyway." The parents did not see themselves that way at all, but it was how their daughter perceived them that determined whether or not she shared. This girl thought she was a disappointment to them and that she "always" let her parents down. "I can see it in their eyes and hear it in their voice." Her memories were not specific but probably referred to sermons and consequences from years ago that were more heavy-handed than they needed to be. We do not want them to keep things inside and we definitely do not want them turning exclusively to their peers for support and advice.

Sometimes the hardest work for parents is to remember *in the heat of the moment* what they know very well at other times. The following exercise can be helpful. Assume you find success at protecting the connection, and with that in mind, write down your thoughts about how your relationship with your children is in the future. Here is one mother's list:

> My children think of me as their biggest fan, not their biggest critic.
> They see me as approachable and non-judgmental.
> They never stop sharing and always turn to me when they are in trouble.
> They discuss issues with me even when they know we will disagree.
> They do not worry about an unexpected emotional outburst from me.
> They feel the security of knowing they can count on me.
> I never lose the ability to teach and guide them.
> They say: "Thanks for the ideas" rather than "You're trying to run my life."

Another mother was keeping a journal during the time we worked together. She would take notes during our sessions and sit at home and write her thoughts whenever there was a tough time. She kept refining her list of "things to remember" and gave this to me to share with other parents:

> Loving my children is not enough, they have to know it.
> How I act today is more important than how they act.
> I am always responsible for my part of the interaction.
> It is up to me whether they will invite me along for their adolescent journey.
> They do not know it, but they are going to need me when they are teenagers.
> Will they perceive me as worthy of their adolescent journey?

> ▸ Will they bless me with their open ears and hearts?
> ▸ My children will have the option to emotionally divorce me.
> ▸ I want them to continue to share with me.
> ▸ They are less likely to do that if I am unable to protect the connection.

I worked with a family where the mother (Susan) had a cancer scare when she was only 40. The cancer was successfully treated and she has been fine for years. She realized during the scariest times, that she parented better than during ordinary times. She truly was able to "be" how she wanted her children to become. After the scare (when she found herself slipping back into her old way of thinking that something was more upsetting than it probably was) she would remember what had been truly frightening, and that helped her get back on track.

Susan's sons were 12 and 15 at the time of her diagnosis. As you can imagine, they were upset and frightened, but they were still 12- and 15-year-old boys. One day the 12-year-old was being particularly obnoxious and self-absorbed and said something to his mother like, "I need you to drive me to John's house right now, come on, right now." She was just about to mirror his inappropriate behavior, but instead found herself smiling and explaining in a soft and loving voice how, whenever he talked to her like that she would say "no" to whatever he wanted. She also reminded him that she could always connect his tone of voice with a consequence, but that she would leave it as a warning for now. She said he stomped off, frustrated, and not at all impressed with her parenting, but she was.

One teenager wrote this before his last family therapy session:

"My parents are crazy about me as I am, not as I could be. Always, not only when all goes well. I am perfect in their eyes exactly the way I am. I make mistakes—like everyone else— and I learn from them. I pay attention to my mistakes and I change and grow. My parents are not disappointed in me. I am not disappointed in myself."

What a helpful reminder about what is important in parenting! It is when our children are not perfect, when we might look or sound disappointed, that we have to protect the connection.

PRESENTING OUR LIVES AS MODELS

Though families use different words and rituals, most keep their faith and religious beliefs at the center of family life. The phrase "living their faith" resonates with families of many faiths and it seems to mean the same thing to everyone. We show children through our actions how we expect them to act as they get older.

Regardless of how badly they are treating us, we treat them better. They are allowed to act their age, but we are not allowed to act *their* age, mirror their insolent tone or "race them to the basement."

There is a higher standard of behavior for us. *We are the adults.* When they are stressful to us, we show them how to act during their own stressful times. One father told me that: "I'm a great parent when my kids aren't around." Another said "I'm a terrific parent except when my kids talk back to me." Eventually it is all about us. *Do we use their behavior as an excuse for our response?* It becomes clear when you say to yourself: *"I want to be the way I want them to become."* Whatever they are doing becomes an opportunity for you to show them how to be.

Michelle was able to be home with her children because of Bob's executive position with a well-known company. He traveled for business once each month, typically for four days. She brought their children to the first therapy session but later came by herself. At first she said she wanted them to listen better, but soon said she wanted to present herself differently when they did not listen well.

Michelle was a delightful person, college educated, outgoing and energetic. Everybody liked her, including her children. But she described herself as "ornery" when ignored. She learned to develop discipline plans for the uncooperative times and to use a quiet voice and a respectful tone. She also learned to view such moments as opportunities to teach her kids about the importance of cooperating with power.

Resilient teenagers typically have parents who taught them that inner calmness is not completely due to life events. Fragile teenagers typically had parents who taught them (unintentionally) that it was only possible to feel good on good days.

Look at it from a child's perspective. Maybe in the first grade, a parent got upset when the child made them late for work and school. In the third grade, the parent "lost it" when toys were not put away. Then in fifth grade, there was nagging about chores and homework. At each age, the parents were perceived by the children as critical, judgmental and hard to please. What children do wrong changes over time, but it is our response at each age that will matter the most.

Can we show them that we can be fine (or at least fine enough) when our day is not perfect? Can we show them we are not angry at them, or disappointed in them, even when they are challenging? Can we remember that they will be less resilient later if we are tense and irritable at stressful times now?

Children need us to be calm when they are being difficult, and also when our own lives outside of the family, are less than perfect. If we come home every day complaining about a delayed project, a boss who does not appreciate us, a sister-in-law or a colleague who said something critical, they might learn that the only times to feel good is when everything is fine. How will they be in fifth grade when a best friend moves away or in seventh grade when a clique of bratty kids teases them? How often is everything fine when you are 14 or 15?

Teaching our children how to deal with stress is something *only we can do*. There are other people who can teach them other things. But what if we take on too many roles?

Some parents tutor their children in math, give them piano lessons, or help them with a sport, and this can occasionally lead to "unnecessary" tension. Unnecessary because math and piano can be taught by others. If we overextend ourselves to help them with math or piano and end up dealing with stress poorly ourselves, it is better to let others help with math or piano, allowing us to do what only parents can do.

Children seem more affected by the times of poor modeling than they are by all of the good. There is a lot at stake, which is why we have to take such good care of ourselves and have realistic priorities of parenting.

Here is the shortest "cheat sheet" about role modeling I have ever seen:

> ➤ Look in the mirror, not across the room.
> ➤ Be in charge of me. Know my buttons. They can try to push them, but they are my buttons.
> ➤ When I feel like I have to control them, control myself.
> ➤ They learn by my model, not my sermons.

The mother who wrote this had another strategy as well. She kept asking herself what would happen if her children became like her at different times during the day: "Now? If they became like me now, would it be OK? How about now?" She said it helped her step back a bit, unplug from the emotions, breathe in, breathe out, and observe without reacting.

If we get cranky when things do not go smoothly, it is probably better to acknowledge that we are not handling our stress very well, and that we have a plan to get back on track, rather than imply that the external events are controlling us. Try not to fret and stew for hours about your less-than-perfect day. The world already has enough teenagers who fret and stew.

Instead, say out loud that feelings pass and there is so much good all around us, anyway. These are the times when we teach that worth is not completely dependent on accomplishments or how many people out there think we are terrific. If the stress was due to a mistake we made, we forgive ourselves and remark: "I'm going to have to work on that." Since they will have their own personal growth plans for many years, we use our life as a model and show them how the personal growth process works.

Try to view everyday stress as an opportunity to demonstrate that our moods are not dependent on the day. *Children learn from us how to be resilient* and to bounce back from whatever happens. A play date gets canceled, a friend moves away, they do not make a high school team, or a first boyfriend or girlfriend breaks up with them abruptly.

After all, in years to come, they will hurt more at times of mistakes and disappointments if they have been watching us be hurt when our lives were not perfect.

STRESS MANAGEMENT

There are the basics of stress management (adequate sleep, eat well, exercise, time to yourself, time with spouse and friends). And there are tips that apply more to our years as parents:

➤ Be careful about how busy the family gets. A family can get too busy to function well. Decide how busy your family can be and still be healthy.

➤ How we spend our time sends a message about our values. If our time is spent away from our children, even when it is devoted to work or volunteer projects, it is still time away. Similarly, if we allow sports to interfere with their homework, we may be sending them a message about what matters most.

➤ If your family is as busy as possible one year, do not add anything next year without subtracting something. Refer back to the "blank week" exercise. Your children need time to relax with you more than any enrichment opportunity.

➤ Know your early warning signs—what it looks and feels like when your stress management plan is beginning to fail.

Just as we may not be at our best when we are stressed, neither are our children. Their capacity for dealing with stress is certainly less than ours, and we will not always know all the details about their stress. We need to be able to forgive ourselves and them for the times when stress gets the best of us. And when a shift is tough, we call it that—a tough shift, rather than thinking that we are a bad parent or that we have bad children. Anything we can do to manage the stress is a gift to our children.

YOU HAVE ALREADY TAUGHT THEM HOW TO DRIVE

One last driving analogy. When teenagers start driving lessons, the parents are told they have already taught their teenager how to drive before their first time behind the wheel. The logic is that they have been in the car with us for years. They watched as we drove at the posted speed and stayed in lane, or drove fast and changed lanes. They watched when we stopped at stop signs or when we rolled through them. It is not so different with the long-term goals. They either watched us be resilient and able to calibrate our emotional reactions to events or not. What have we already taught them? When we model, we teach.

NOT WHAT THEY DO

Parents are typically concerned about the wrong things. If the children steal at 6, will they grow up to be thieves? But what if it is not *their* current behavior that predicts their future behavior but *our* current behavior that affects their future behavior?

That brings us back to the blind spots. It makes more sense for parents to be concerned about how their blind spots interfere with their modeling. Honoring sovereignty. Protecting the connection. Disciplining with reassurance. These seem to be the better predictors of our children's future behavioral or emotional struggles. What they present us with when they are 6 is most likely 6-year-old behavior.

Imagine a parent describing their teenage son's anger management problem, with the specifics of the latest incident. The parent relates that this has been a problem for years: "He has always been this way." While there is always nature and nurture (genetics and environment), parenting is the bridge between the two. Consider the different answers to the following question: What was happening five minutes before the son had his anger management problem? If the answer is a definitive "Nothing, he just exploded," then perhaps we understand the problem as more likely influenced by genetics. If the answer is very different, highlighting comments, gestures and demands by both parent and son, with a gradual escalation until finally the son exploded, we understand the problem as more likely influenced by the environment and the parenting. And what if *that pattern* has always been this way?

When it seems as if they have always been a certain way (sensitive, easily hurt, perfectionistic, stubborn or headstrong) consider nature and nurture. If you can see a pattern where your blind spots led you to miss teaching opportunities, and if that explains what your children have not yet learned, direct some effort in that direction. The good news, of course, is that the smaller the role of genetics, the better chance that our children will change as we change and follow us into the future.

THE TWO COUCHES

As was discussed in Chapter One, the impetus for this book was my work with teenagers and their parents in therapy. We end up with a teenager on one couch and the parents on the other couch, wondering how they got there. This section connects frequently occurring reasons for teenagers to be in therapy with certain parent characteristics.

There are very real disadvantages to broad generalizations. In some ways, no two families are ever alike. However, after the individuality of each teenager and parent, and the unique circumstances of each family's life has been considered, some patterns still remain.

The following is a summary of some commonly observed patterns in therapy. As you read this section, keep the blind spots in mind.

Parents often bring their teenager in for one of the following reasons:

> Low self-esteem, clingy, dependent, unsure of themselves, hesitant to try new things.
> Underachieving, poor effort/attitude, no "value" of education.
> Gloomy, negative, isolates, withdraws from family, pessimism.
> Lies, withholds information, manipulates, blames others, does not take responsibility.
> Burst into adolescence, rude, obnoxious, backtalk, temper outbursts.
> Wrong crowd, risk-taking, adventure-seeking, sexually active, lack of caution, irrational sense of invulnerability.
> Sense of entitlement, too powerful, cocky, arrogant, boastful, uncompromising, wants to drive their own life but they are not steering.
> Obsessive worrying, reviews, rehashes and rehearses.
> Perfectionism, eating disorders, depression.

Each will be reviewed with an emphasis on how the parents and their blind spots may have contributed to the teenager's problems.

Low self-esteem, clingy, dependent, unsure of themselves, hesitant to try new things

Parents who struggled with boundary problems and tried to help too much, especially when their children were in third, fourth and fifth grade often ended up with teenagers who struggled with low self-esteem, were unsure of themselves and hesitant to try new things. This makes sense because the over-helping robbed the children of opportunities to tackle new experiences, as well as to experience some failures and some successes, and learn from both. On the other hand, parents who were judging and highly critical of everyday life contributed to a deep-seated lack of confidence in their children. Some teenagers have memories of feeling as if they were not meeting one or both parent's expectations. How can those teenagers face their day with confidence with those memories? In addition, too much worrying about dreadful but extremely rare events such as being abducted, or too much of a focus on the world as an unfair and unforgiving place seemed to contribute as well.

Underachieving, poor effort/attitude, no "value" of education

Some children love learning for its own sake and love to please their teachers and parents. Others learn the value of education by their parents connecting whatever is important to them with school performance. Some underachieving teenagers had parents who intruded or hesitated to act, threatened but did not follow through, or pulled back for a while and then roared back to help with anger and a rescuing mentality. There were too many words, not enough action. They did not allow their children to earn their own grades and they did not connect poor grades with loss of privileges. Well-intentioned parents may have been in constant communication with teachers through phone, email or school website portals, thus inadvertently depriving their children of developing those skills themselves. Academics became a parent-child issue, with interpersonal tension and regrettable scenes.

Gloomy, negative, isolates, withdraws from family, pessimism

When there was negativity and withdrawal from family life, there was often a pattern of parents who were not able to honor their children's sovereignty. Children were compared to standards, and the pessimism followed years of parent nagging and criticizing. Sometimes the teenagers never learned to deal with ordinary disappointments and now had trouble feeling good except on perfect days, or the parents had tried to cheer the younger children up too much, rather than teaching them how to view the normal disappointments of childhood.

Lies, withholds information, manipulates, blames others, does not take responsibility

For the most part, this cluster of behavior was associated with extremes of parenting. On the one hand, parents who were gullible, naïve, and overly trusting or who acted like the parent-child relationship was one of equals, seemed to be on the one couch when their teenager was on the other couch. An inconsistent approach, perhaps because of parental disagreement seemed to be present as well. On the other hand, parents who used consequences that were too big or too long-lasting, disciplining with anger rather than reassurance, inadvertently taught the children to lie.

Burst into adolescence, rude, obnoxious, backtalk, temper outbursts

One pattern was the parent who modeled that it was acceptable for "big people" to speak disrespectfully, but not for "little people." Parents who raced their children to the basement, and mirrored them at their worst, contributed as well. There were too many angry moments, too much tension, too many explanations, and a tendency to over-psychologize.

Wrong crowd, risk-taking, adventure-seeking, sexually active, lack of caution, irrational sense of invulnerability

These teenagers often had parents who were over-protective in earlier years. Some had a "bubble childhood," filled with warnings about not climbing trees or riding their bicycle on gravel roads. In addition, parents may have taught that "lines move for us." If the children were late with an assignment, the teacher was asked to accept it the next day without penalty. The children may have been coddled and deprived of ordinary lessons of actions and natural consequences, with the unintended result that they now felt above the fray, almost invulnerable to ordinary danger.

Sense of entitlement, too powerful, cocky, arrogant, boastful, uncompromising, wants to drive own life (but not steering)

What seems harmless early in childhood seems different in adolescence. Parents who worshipped their children, considering them uniquely talented, whether due to academic, athletic, art, singing, or dance ability, sometimes were too timid and reluctant to hold them accountable. As adolescence approached, parents might have allowed overnights at friends' homes without calling the other parents to make sure there would be proper supervision. Or they might have accepted as true the tale about "just holding the cigarettes (or beer or marijuana) for a friend." Later, when their child is in high school, they might grant freedoms on weekends without insisting on the details.

Obsessive worrying, reviews, rehashes and rehearses

More often than not, this cluster is reminiscent of the apple that did not fall far from the tree. These teenagers typically had parents who did not teach about closure, repeatedly brought up the same issues, sermonized past the point of diminishing returns. Problems at bedtime at 6, 7, or 8 were worsened by parents who tried to help by staying up with the children, asking insight-oriented questions and in general modeling a ruminative approach to life's problems. With an obsessive teenager on one couch, it was not a surprise to see parents on the other couch who were overly self-critical when they made mistakes, and crumbly when life was disappointing.

Perfectionism, eating disorders, depression

How good do I have to be to be good enough? Teenagers who found it hard to be comfortable in their own skin, often had parents who had not been able to teach them that worth and self-esteem is supposed to be based on core values and inner principles rather than merely grades, chores, manners, or athletic ability. These parents missed moments to teach resilience, typically because they overemphasized the striving, achievement or weight and appearance issues.

These brief descriptions are not definitive by any means but are included to help lay the foundation for the next section. As you will see, there are many moments every day that can be used to teach young children what they will need when they are older.

Chapter 8

Making
Moments Count

This chapter describes how to use the everyday moments of family life to prepare children for their future. As you will see, it builds on previous chapters, especially the long-term goals, mistakes and disappointments, and blind spots. A table is provided at the beginning of each section to help you see what mistakes and disappointments are going to be discussed for each age group. These tables will also be helpful when you refer back to this chapter as your children get older.

Since I wanted to include many examples, this chapter may seem a bit daunting at first. Be sure to notice the parentheses with the prompt about the blind spots and do not hesitate to refer back to that chapter. In fact, the two segments about blind spots in Chapter Four ("Does this blind spot affect you?" and "What to do about it") may even be more helpful now, with the examples. Table One, from Chapter One, is reprinted at the end of this chapter, to help you track the specific teaching opportunities (e.g., knowing what worth is based on) that contribute to the long-term goals (e.g., resilience).

For each age group, preschool, kindergarten—second grade, third—fifth grade, sixth—eighth grade, and high school, normal everyday moments of childhood are organized into mistakes and disappointments. While not an exhaustive list, it demonstrates how to find possible teaching opportunities in everyday family life. The moments included are the ones parents ask most about. Organizing them into mistakes and disappointments helps in two ways:

1. If your child is experiencing one of the listed mistakes or disappointments, you immediately have an example of how to proceed. But you will also get ideas about how to deal with other mistakes and disappointments. Perhaps the approach recommended will provide ideas for the challenges your children are presenting you with now.

2. This also highlights the blind spots. Pay close attention to the mistakes and disappointments that have been difficult for you, especially the times you parented in a way you later regretted. These experiences are the ones that will help you learn about your own blind spots. When you understand why you were not able to see the teaching opportunity, you may learn something important about yourself that will help you improve your parenting. This will matter a great deal because even though we cannot always influence our children's present as much as we would like, we will certainly influence their future by how we parent each day.

As you will see, this approach further explores the ideas presented in the chapters on *honoring sovereignty, disciplining with reassurance, protecting the connection and presenting our lives as models.* At times it uses a narrative style, written as a parent would speak to a child, because the words can be elusive at first, even after this approach is understood.

Just as the preschool years lay the foundation for all the years to come, the preschool chapter lays the foundation for all the sections to come. It is written differently than the others and provides more narrative examples. All parents are encouraged to read it even if your youngest child has already started school.

The format for this chapter is as follows:

MOMENT   A specific mistake or disappointment.
LONG-TERM GOAL A teaching opportunity. (See Table One)

Honoring sovereignty:

› Examples of words to use that convey how we honor their sovereignty.

Disciplining with reassurance:

› Consequences for the discipline, tone of voice for the reassurance.

Protecting the connection:

› Ways to strengthen their sense of security with us right in the moment.

Presenting our lives as models:

› Reminders about how every moment is a chance for us to model for them how we hope they become.

PRESCHOOL MISTAKES AND LONG-TERM GOALS

Preschool Mistakes	Long-term Goal: Resilience
Morning routine, getting out of the house on time.	What worth is based on
Does not want to try new things, accidents, bedwetting.	Self-esteem is not contingent on a smooth road
Finicky eater.	Anticipate disappointments

Preschool Mistakes	Long-term Goal: Emotional Calibration
Young child says "I hate you" to the parent. Acts snotty or whiny.	Thoughts precede feelings
Hits (bites) a peer in day care.	Learn about sizing

Preschool Mistakes	Long-term Goal: Interpersonal Skills
Trouble falling asleep, vague physical complaints.	Boundaries and self-advocacy
We find food in their room, and they say it is not theirs.	That trust is important
Behavior problems in public, meltdowns, tantrums, does not play well with friend on a play date, does not take turns.	Personal growth process
Difficulties with siblings, teasing, fighting.	Communication and conflict resolution skills
When kids are selfish, self-centered, trouble sharing.	Compassion

Inappropriate behavior at mealtimes, not coming when called, not staying seated, making silly noises.	Internal locus of control
Sibling gets all the attention because of a birthday or sports event. Have to wait (e.g., delayed at airport, get frustrated easily).	Stress management

Preschool Mistakes	Long-term Goal: Connected to Us
They say: "You're the meanest mom in the whole world" or "everyone else can do it." Wears ridiculous clothes. Lies to us.	Perceive us accurately as their reservoir of confidence
Bedtime routine, brushing their teeth, meal time, bath time. Putting toys away, making their bed, keeping their room clean.	Logical consequences given in a loving and forgiving way by relaxed parents

MOMENT	Morning routine, getting out of the house on time.
LONG-TERM GOAL	Resilience: What worth is based on

Since so many parents have a hard time getting their preschoolers out the door in the morning, let us use this moment to describe in detail the layout for this chapter. Viewing the morning routine as an opportunity to teach about resilience and what worth is based on helps us know how to proceed.

It goes without saying that paying attention to time, cooperating with us and getting moving are all important. But we do not want to make things worse in our efforts to make them better. We want this problem to end as soon as it can and not become a long-standing source of parent-child tension.

When we *honor their sovereignty,* we view this as a mistake and one that many preschoolers make. If one of our worrying blind spots is interfering, we might have a short fuse and perhaps project linearly, anticipate this continuing for years if we do not "nip it in the bud". The judging blind spots might lead us to compare to an unrealistic standard (e.g., preschoolers should always cooperate with parents), and then we might act in an angry or impatient way. Instead our tone is soothing and the words we use let them know we are confident that together we will figure this out:

> ▸ "Mornings seem hard for you, maybe tomorrow will be better."
> ▸ "A lot of 4-year-olds have trouble getting out the door in the morning."
> ▸ "This is exactly the kind of mistake I expect from you at this age."
> ▸ "Everybody makes mistakes, that's how people learn."
> ▸ "You are right on time, acting exactly like a 4-year-old."

The *disciplining with reassurance* might include a chart as part of your behavior plan. They could earn a sticker when they are ready on time, and the stickers could add up to a favorite game or a special date with you on the weekend. We put the plan in place with a reassuring voice:

> ► "We'll get through this together for as long as it takes."
> ► "This isn't my favorite thing but it isn't the end of the world."
> ► "Maybe there's something you need to learn that can only be taught at a time like this."

Protecting the connection reminds you to hold them close and say something soothing instead of a response that adds distance to the parent-child relationship. The following examples may be too mushy to say out loud for some parents, but comfortable for others. I am including them primarily because we might say them to ourselves even if we do not want to say them to our children. Whatever you decide to say, remember that any parent can discipline harshly, but it takes effort to discipline and protect the connection at the same time.

> ► "This isn't your finest moment."
> ► "Even with this mistake you're still perfect in my eyes."
> ► "I still love you. It's just a mistake you're making and I am here to help."
> ► "Now I get to get to be close to you while you work on your morning routine."

Finally, *presenting our lives as models* clarifies that there is nothing about being late that has to make us feel or act a certain way. In fact, since it can be stressful it gives us a chance to show our children how we handle this stress.

> ➤ "Now I get to help you with your morning problem."
> ➤ "Let's see what we can learn from this that maybe can only be learned from a moment like this."
> ➤ "Now you get to learn how it feels when you make this kind of a mistake."
> ➤ "I have some ideas on how we can work this out."
> ➤ "What do you think we can do to make this better?"

This approach takes a routine event and turns it into an opportunity to teach about resilience. Our focus stays on the behavior we want to change, and we also send clear messages that our children's worth has nothing to do with this mistake they are making. If our blind spots got in our way, if we were not able to honor their sovereignty, discipline with reassurance, protect the connection and present our lives as models, this everyday moment would have a very different outcome. A child could get yelled at day after day by a frustrated parent. After a while, instead of learning that their worth is unaffected by their mistakes, they might learn a very different lesson altogether.

MOMENT	Does not want to try new things, accidents, bedwetting.
LONG-TERM GOAL	Resilience: Self-esteem is not contingent on a smooth road

Preschool children vary in their sense of security, their willingness to explore and their physical development. Some are clumsy during the day, knocking things over, spilling their drinks and breaking household items. Others do not realize they have to go to the bathroom until it is too late. By "starting where they are at," we develop a plan to help them and avoid the *judging* blind spots.

How big are these problems for our children? It probably depends on how *we* size them more than anything. Our children will most likely follow our emotional lead. If we are worried either because they are missing out on fun or they might be embarrassed, they might sense our concern and be affected by our reaction. However, if instead of trying to fix things and change them "as soon as possible" we use this moment to teach that life includes setbacks, missed opportunities and disappointments, we will know exactly how we want to proceed.

Honoring sovereignty:

➤ "Your body is developing at exactly the right pace for you."

➤ "It's OK to skip this birthday party. Maybe you'll want to go to the next one."

➤ "Nobody's perfect, even mommy and daddy make mistakes."

Disciplining with reassurance:

➤ "To help you learn to move more carefully at home, when you break something your consequence will be to help me fold towels on laundry day."

Protecting the connection:

➤ "I'm not mad at you because you wet your bed. It happens."

➤ "You're a terrific kid when you break things and when you don't."

➤ "Oh well, everybody spills something once in a while. Let's clean it up together."

MOMENT   Finicky eater.

LONG-TERM GOAL   Resilience: Anticipate disappointments

It is unlikely that younger children described as finicky eaters will become older children diagnosed with serious eating problems. In fact, parents who make a fuss about what is served or eaten may be complicating things unnecessarily. What if the long-term goal was simply to help our children deal with the disappointment of not getting what they want? There should be no special meal preparation and no tension about what they eat or do not eat. The *intruding* blind spots can make this hard to see.

Honoring sovereignty:

> ➤ "You are in charge of what you eat, but you're not in charge of what I serve."
> ➤ "You might be hungry later, but you can always help yourself to an apple or a peanut butter and jelly sandwich."
> ➤ "It's not the end of the world, lots of kids are fussy about food from time to time."

Protecting the connection:

> ➤ "I understand you wish I was making something else for dinner."
> ➤ "Thank you for sharing your feelings but your whining hurts my ears."

Presenting our lives as models:

> ➤ We can be calm and show them by our model that we are unflappable.
> ➤ We can show them that we know where we end and where they begin, that we cannot crawl inside of them and make sure they are always comfortable in every possible way.

MOMENT	Young child says "I hate you" to the parent, or acts snotty or whiny.
LONG-TERM GOAL	Emotional calibration: Thoughts precede feelings

While it does not surprise parents that their children occasionally say something they do not mean or act in a bratty way, it can still be worrisome. "Is my child under some terrible stress? What does it mean when he says these things or acts this way?" Rather than focusing on figuring it out, getting it to stop or helping them feel better right away, maybe this moment is best viewed as an opportunity to teach about feelings in general and the role of thoughts in particular. During preschool we might have to guess about the thoughts that might be affecting their feelings and provide these as prompts. This work will be ongoing, and progress will not be evident for many years. If this is hard to see, it might be because of the *worrying* (especially over-psychologizing) or the *intruding* (myth of the smooth road) blind spots.

Honoring sovereignty:

- "You sound very upset. Here's another way to let me know that you're upset."
- "If you use these words instead, you can still tell me you're angry without getting yourself into trouble."

Disciplining with reassurance:

- "It's not acceptable when you speak to me like that. Early bed for you tonight."
- "You know I have to give a consequence when you act this way."
- "No cooperation means no friend over."

Protecting the connection:

- "Even though you're mad at me, I'm not mad at you."
- "Maybe it's because you had such a long day and that's why you're so crabby."
- "We'll learn from this—tomorrow we won't plan such a busy day."

Presenting our lives as models:

- When we show them we are unworried, it is calming and reassuring for them.
- This is a chance to be at our best when they are not at their best.

MOMENT Hits (bites) a peer in day care.

LONG-TERM GOAL Emotional calibration: Learn about sizing

Usually this kind of behavior problem stems from the child viewing an event as bigger than it really is. Maybe the other child was loud or bossy, racing to be first in line, or took something without asking. While we want to reduce the chances of this happening again, we also want to teach frustration tolerance and how even young children can begin to learn that they have a choice in how they view and react to unpleasant parts of their day. The *worrying* blind spots (especially overly emotional and sizing), might make it hard to remember that these mistakes are a normal part of childhood.

Honoring sovereignty:

- ➤ "I understand you were frustrated."
- ➤ "We'll help you learn new ways to control yourself when you're frustrated."
- ➤ "Lots of children have struggled with this, and they learned not to make this mistake and so will you."
- ➤ "Here's what to say to yourself next time another child is bugging you."

Disciplining with reassurance:

- ➤ Discipline might include one of the following for a day or two: Time outs, early bed, no television, no friend over.
- ➤ A chart can be developed that rewards counting to ten, walking away, asking for help from the teacher.

Protecting the connection:

- ➤ "Yes, this is a mistake and we'll get through this together."
- ➤ "It's not the end of the world."
- ➤ "This is why children have parents for so many years, so their parents can help them learn from these kinds of mistakes."

Presenting our lives as models:
- › Bring home stories from our less-than-perfect lives.
- › Talk about how we handled a stressful moment from our day.
- › Find a chance to talk about how we choose to view a boastful co-worker or a pushy salesperson.

MOMENT	Trouble falling asleep, vague physical complaints.
LONG-TERM GOAL	Interpersonal skills: Boundaries and self-advocacy

It is confusing to us when our children have trouble falling asleep or complain about stomachaches or headaches. If there is not a medical problem, this might provide an opportunity to teach about boundaries. As in previous examples, this work begins during pre-school but it is ongoing.

We want to support them and comfort them and at the same time clarify for them that we cannot solve this problem for them. Ideas and suggestions we have, but magic power to make this go away we do not have. The parents who over-help (*intruding* blind spot) seem to handle this kind of problem in a way that perpetuates it rather than resolves it.

Honoring sovereignty:
- › "I'm glad to know about this problem you're having, thanks for telling me."
- › "You'll figure this out at your own schedule, between now and then you'll be OK. All that happens if you don't sleep well tonight is that you'll be a little tired tomorrow."
- › "A little tummy ache or a crummy night sleep isn't our favorite thing, but it's not a huge catastrophe either."

Protecting the connection:

- ➤ "I'll rub your back for ten minutes, maybe you'll fall asleep before I leave."
- ➤ "If you're still up, you can listen to your special music and practice your breathing exercises."

Presenting our lives as models:

- ➤ The house is peaceful, and we begin moving slower as bed time approaches.
- ➤ We do what we can to have time with them before bedtime so they do not have reason to try to extend the bedtime routine to have more time with us.
- ➤ Maybe we volunteer for one less thing and turn the television and computer off earlier than usual to allow time to read with them.

MOMENT	We find food in their room, and they say it is not theirs.
LONG-TERM GOAL	Interpersonal skills: That trust is important

It is so easy for the *judging* blind spots to interfere (e.g., comparisons to invisible rulebooks) with our ability to teach at times of such obvious mistakes. Of course they should not lie to us, and yes, food in their room could invite bugs. However, this can be an opening to talk about how important trust is in relationships.

Honoring sovereignty:

- ➤ "It is a mistake to lie to me about food in your room."
- ➤ "It's confusing for me when I'm not sure if I can trust you."
- ➤ "Trust leads to freedoms and privileges. Without my trust you'll miss out on fun times."

Disciplining with reassurance:

> ➤ "You need to take responsibility for your mistake by writing me a note (or drawing me a picture)."
> ➤ Extra cleaning chores, dishes, wiping the counter, might all be fitting consequences.

Protecting the connection:

> ➤ "I love you when you tell the truth and when you lie."
> ➤ "When you lie, you get a consequence, but that's all that happens."
> ➤ "Kids your age aren't perfect (and neither are your parents)."

Presenting our lives as models:

> ➤ It is stressful when they lie to us, so we can show them how we handle stress at those times.
> ➤ We can say out loud how we are choosing to view their mistake in the way that keeps us calm.

MOMENT	Behavior problems in public, meltdowns, tantrums, does not play well with friend on a play date, does not take turns.
LONG-TERM GOAL	Interpersonal skills: Personal growth process

Every child needs to learn about the personal growth process, how to set goals, acknowledge need areas, and make improvements. While it is never fun when our children are having meltdowns in public or not playing well with a friend, we can at least view them as opportunities to introduce this important part of life. Some parents have trouble seeing their children's shortcomings if the *hesitating* blind spots (especially the "worship" one) interfere.

Honoring sovereignty:
- ➤ "Your behavior wasn't acceptable."
- ➤ "We will start working on it today and keep working on it for as long as it takes."

Disciplining with reassurance:
- ➤ "We won't be able to go out together for a few days because of the way you acted."
- ➤ "I'm not mad at you, but your behavior needs to change."
- ➤ "Here's how you can earn the privilege of going out with me again."

Protecting the connection:
- ➤ We move slowly and talk softly even while they are difficult.
- ➤ If we have to leave a grocery cart in a supermarket or a department store and cut our losses, that is what we will do.

Presenting our lives as models:
- ➤ We do not have to feel embarrassed if they meltdown in public, only if we meltdown in public.
- ➤ Show them we can be patient, wait until we get home and then develop and follow through with a discipline plan.

MOMENT	Difficulties with siblings, teasing, fighting.
LONG-TERM GOAL	Interpersonal skills: Communication and conflict resolution skills

If you have more than one child, you will have sibling problems, and they will provide many opportunities to teach communication and conflict resolution skills. The *worrying* (overly emotional, and low tolerance for conflict) and the *intruding* (myth of the smooth road and over-help) blind spots seem to get in the way the most.

Honoring sovereignty:

> - Our children are in a relationship with each other that we cannot completely control.
> - Remember that sisters and brothers being unkind to each other is a universal problem that has existed for as long as any of us can imagine.

Disciplining with reassurance:

> - Try to avoid taking on the role as mediator especially if it is hard for you to avoid the trap of viewing the younger sibling as an innocent victim.
> - Most often if discipline is needed, it is best to give the same consequence to both children rather than siding with one over the other.

Protecting the connection:

> - By sitting with them and helping them both say what they need to say, their listening skills will gradually improve.
> - The trap to avoid is inserting ourselves into the conflict and robbing them of the teaching opportunity.

Presenting our lives as models:

> - Sometimes their bickering is more stressful for us than it is for them.
> - We can show them how we stay calm even when one or both of them is being challenging.
> - Hang on to the idea that things will get better as long as we do nothing to make things worse.

MOMENT	When kids are selfish, self-centered, trouble sharing.
LONG-TERM GOAL	Interpersonal skills: Compassion

Usually it is the *worrying* (projecting linearly) and the *judging* (invisible rulebook) blind spots that make it hard for parents to see this as an opportunity to teach compassion. If we get blinded by "What will they be like when they are older?" or "They should not be acting this way at this age," our actions will probably make things worse rather than better.

Honoring sovereignty:
> ▸ "We'll get through this together."
> ▸ "This is how kids your age learn how good it feels to share."

Disciplining with reassurance:
> ▸ "If you're having trouble sharing, maybe it's because you have too much stuff."
> ▸ "Let's put a few things away for a few weeks—maybe that will help you learn to share."
> ▸ "Remember how good it felt last week when your cousins let you play with their toys."

Protecting the connection:
> ▸ As long as we stay away from, "There you go again. How many times do I have to tell you to share your toys," we will be fine.

Presenting our lives as models:
> ▸ They see our compassion towards them at the time they are selfish and self-centered, and we know that in time they will become more like us.

MOMENT	Inappropriate behavior at mealtimes, not coming when called, not staying seated, making silly noises.
LONG-TERM GOAL	Interpersonal skills: Internal locus of control

When they do not listen to us or follow our directions, they need a consequence. However, silly noises and other inappropriate behavior at mealtimes are not likely to lead to any serious problems in years to come. All we have to watch out for is how we respond. Parents seem to like the idea that these moments are perfect exactly the way they are because children need to develop their self-control skills. How else would they develop these skills if not for times like these? If we fail to see the need for discipline because of the *hesitating* blind spots, then our lack of response could contribute to later problems.

Honoring sovereignty:

> ➤ "Mealtimes are hard for you, and they bring out the sillies."

Disciplining with reassurance:

> ➤ "When you act like this, you will be given a consequence."
> ➤ "Please remember that even things you take for granted, like television or having friends over, are privileges that can be connected with your behavior."
> ➤ "I'll take one thing for one day and we'll see if that helps."

Protecting the connection:

> ➤ We start where they are at and help them.
> ➤ We do not make things worse by our response.

Presenting our lives as models:

> ➤ They are reassured by our soft voice and our calmness even when they are making their mistake.

MOMENT	Sibling gets all the attention because of a birthday or sports event. Have to wait (e.g., delayed at airport, get frustrated easily).
LONG-TERM GOAL	Interpersonal skills: Stress management

Life includes stress even for our preschoolers, and those are the times when they begin the life-long lessons about stress management. The *intruding* (myth of the smooth road, over-help) blind spots sometimes lead parents to try heroic measures to keep their children happy and comfortable at all times rather than teaching what can be taught. Sometimes the *worrying* (overly emotional, over-psychologizing) blind spots make things more complicated than they need to be.

Honoring sovereignty:

- ▸ "Yes, you're right. Today is your sister's birthday and she gets all the attention."
- ▸ "When it's your birthday you get all the attention, but not today."

Disciplining with reassurance:

- ▸ "This is a normal part of life and a chance for you to work on feeling OK even when life isn't perfect."
- ▸ "If your behavior isn't acceptable, you will be held responsible even though it is your sister's birthday, no excuses."

Protecting the connection:

- ▸ As always, we treat them better than they deserve, better than they are treating us.

Presenting our lives as models:

- ▸ "Since we're stuck at the airport anyway, let's take turns between reading stories and going exploring."

MOMENT	They say: "You're the meanest mom in the whole world" or "everybody else can do it." Wears ridiculous clothes. Lies to us.
LONG-TERM GOAL	Connected to us: Perceive us accurately as their reservoir of confidence

While these mistakes are not of great concern, their frequency allows us to continually present ourselves as a source of stability and confidence for our preschoolers. Since we can choose to view these moments as harmless, we can observe them without reacting. When children see their parents day after day as calm and reassuring they are comforted and more likely to stay closely connected. The *intruding* (especially parenting as cloning and poor listener when they try to help) blind spots can interfere.

Honoring sovereignty:
- ➤ "I understand that you're angry with me right now."
- ➤ "Children can love their parents and be angry with them at the same time."

Protecting the connection:
- ➤ "You may wear that bulky jacket today, just so you know it's going to be warm later."
- ➤ "Some parents let their children do this, but in our family we don't, and we don't compare."

Presenting our lives as models:
- ➤ Our ability to stay calm during the small daily times when our preschoolers are adding small tension to the day is a great gift to our children.
- ➤ They will not remember what they were doing, but they will remember how we responded.

MOMENT	Bedtime routine, brushing their teeth, meal time, bath time. Putting toys away, making their bed, keeping their room clean.
LONG-TERM GOAL	Connected to us: Logical consequences given in a loving and forgiving way by re-laxed parents

Some of the smallest moments can be used to teach. Most parents struggle with their children on issues of daily cooperation. As long as we avoid the *judging* and the *hesitating* blind spots, it is clear that these challenges permit us to introduce our children to logical consequences and our style of parenting at such times. Since this will be a "dance" between parent and child for many years, we might as well create a peaceful and loving one.

Honoring sovereignty:
- ➤ "You have choices. If you cooperate with me you will have more privileges and fewer consequences."
- ➤ "I can't make you put your toys away, but if you don't, I will put them away for a few days."

Disciplining with reassurance:
- ➤ "It is not my favorite thing when you tell me you brushed your teeth and the toothbrush is dry."
- ➤ "Let's brush our teeth together, and there will be no story for you tonight."

Protecting the connection:
- ➤ "This is why children need parents."
- ➤ "We'll learn from this together."

Presenting our lives as models:
- ➤ When our children are this young, how we are during the difficult moments will either be frightening or reassuring.
- ➤ It may not seem like it, but being calm when they are stressful is everything.

PRESCHOOL DISAPPOINTMENTS AND LONG-TERM GOALS

Preschool Disappointments	Long-term Goal: Resilience
Crying when they lose or miss out on something, crushed by smallest disappointment.	What worth is based on
Play date gets canceled, sibling gets sick and you cannot drive him to the park.	Anticipate disappointments
Transitions, hard to start something new, does not want something to end.	Self-esteem is not contingent on a smooth road

Preschool Disappointments	Long-term Goal: Emotional Calibration
Lose a special object, a new toy breaks. Talks about joining Grandpa in heaven.	Language of feelings
Parent goes on business trip and children are sobbing and having trouble sleeping.	Closure
World events, something they see or hear on the local news. Pet runs away or dies, medical scares.	Optimism, change and loss

Preschool Disappointments	Long-term Goal: Interpersonal Skills
Separation anxiety, cries at daycare or with babysitter.	Boundaries and self-advocacy
A peer takes something that belongs to your child, gets in front of them on line.	Boundaries and self-advocacy

MOMENT	Crying when they lose or miss out on something, crushed by smallest disappointment.
LONG-TERM GOAL	Resilience: What worth is based on

When our children are disappointed, our instinct is to make them feel better right away. When we can comfort or redirect them, it feels right. But we also view the everyday disappointments as opportunities to teach that they are a normal part of life and are to be expected. The *worrying* (overly emotional, sizing) and *intruding* (myth of the smooth road, poor listener) blind spots can interfere.

Honoring sovereignty:

> ▸ "I understand that you are disappointed."
> ▸ "Thank you for sharing your feelings with me."
> ▸ "I always feel close to you when you tell me your feelings."

Protecting the connection:

> ▸ "Now I get to help you with this."
> ▸ "Now I get to show you that this too is part of life."

Presenting our lives as models:

> ▸ "It's a normal part of life to be disappointed."
> ▸ By taking their setbacks in stride we model a way for them to view their setbacks as well.

MOMENT	Play date gets canceled, sibling gets sick and you cannot drive him to the park.
LONG-TERM GOAL	Resilience: Anticipate disappointments

The most resilient teenagers view their disappointments in one way, and the least resilient ones view them in a different way. When we handle cancellations and postponements to teach our young children how to view such events, we are able to do much more than merely cheer them up. The *worrying* and *intruding* blind spots can interfere, but the *judging* ones might lead to parent anger or impatience that is out of proportion with the original problem.

Honoring sovereignty:
- "How may I help you with this?"
- "This is hard for you now. We will work on this together."

Protecting the connection:
- "This is what parents do. It is what families are for."
- "Parents help kids when they have these kinds of problems."

Presenting our lives as models:
- Who we are when the plan for our day changes will help them more than anything.
- Think of this when you have car trouble.

MOMENT	Transitions, hard to start something new, does not want something to end.
LONG-TERM GOAL	Resilience: Self-esteem is not contingent on a smooth road

Preschoolers have trouble with transitions, and there are many transitions for many years. They feel comfortable with what they are doing and they are not sure about what is next. Viewing these moments as opportunities to teach the difference between how we feel and how our day is going can help them when they are older. With our help they learn how to bring their inner strength with them to the next adventure. You may need to be careful about the *worrying* (overly emotional, sizing) blind spots causing you to see this age-appropriate problem as a sign of a more serious problem.

Honoring sovereignty:

> ➤ "I understand that you want to keep doing what you're doing."
> ➤ "Thank you for sharing your feelings with me."
> ➤ "Lots of kids your age have a hard time with this. You'll be fine."

Disciplining with reassurance:

> ➤ Some moments arrive with their own need to be managed. They still provide a teaching opportunity, but it might be deferred. The time for discipline sometimes comes later, when they are calmer.
> ➤ A chart devoted to how they handle transitions can give us an easy way to reward them for improved behavior.

Protecting the connection:

> ➤ We do not follow their lead.
> ➤ They are allowed their feelings even if it includes crying and screaming.

Presenting our lives as models:

> ➤ Even if they tantrum, we can stay calm and show them how they will act when they are older (like us!).

MOMENT	Lose a special object, a new toy breaks. Talks about joining Grandpa in heaven.
LONG-TERM GOAL	Emotional calibration: Language of feelings

The theme here is feelings. Grandparents die, and things break or get lost. Feelings pour out of preschoolers, and we do not have to be alarmed (even if they say they want to die so they can be with Grandpa). We use the sadness and everyday losses to teach them about how it helps to share feelings and how feelings change from day to day. The *worrying* (over-psychologizing) blind spot can interfere.

Honoring sovereignty:

- ➤ "It makes sense that you would feel that way, thanks for sharing."
- ➤ "Even though you feel this way today, you'll probably feel differently tomorrow."

Protecting the connection:

- ➤ "This is why children have parents for so many years."
- ➤ "For now we miss Grandpa. We'll see him again when the time is right for us to see him."

Presenting our lives as models:

- ➤ They learn from watching us when we have our losses.
- ➤ Bring home stories of small losses from your day away from them and create teaching moments.
- ➤ If you lose a purse or a set of keys, you can show them how you handle your feelings.

MOMENT	Parent goes on business trip and children are sobbing and having trouble sleeping.
LONG-TERM GOAL	Emotional calibration: Closure

It makes perfect sense that they would miss us and have a hard time when we are gone. Instead of just trying to solve the immediate problem, we can also teach about closure. Our children will need to be able to comfort themselves as they move through childhood, and one needed skill is to know how to stop the line of thinking that is causing the stress. The *worrying* (projecting linearly) and *intruding* (over-help) blind spots can interfere.

Honoring sovereignty:

- ➤ "I miss Mommy too, but we'll be fine."
- ➤ "An action plan will help. Maybe we can plan a lot of activity during the day and stay up later so you'll be really tired and have an easier time falling to sleep."

> ➤ "Let's talk about our feelings while the sun is up, and at night let's draw pictures and read stories."

Protecting the connection:

> ➤ By not getting too concerned about this and not thinking we have to make them feel better immediately, we can be connected to them and comfort them by our presence.

Presenting our lives as models:

> ➤ When we have something on our minds, we can show them how we decide when to think about it and how to put it on a shelf for another day when we are ready.
> ➤ They can learn about breathing and relaxation exercises, yoga or meditation from us.

MOMENT	World events, something they see or hear on the local news Pet runs away or dies, medical scares.
LONG-TERM GOALS	Emotional calibration: Optimism, change and loss

Sometimes it seems as if keeping the television off most of the time would be a reasonable parenting strategy, especially with how upsetting the news can be. Even so, the best approach for these kinds of times is to teach about optimism and how much goes right in the world every day that never makes it to the newspaper or the television news programs. And, since we know that change and loss are part of life, we use what comes up to teach our children the skills they will need for their whole lives. It almost always helps children to have accurate information shared with them in a timely manner. That way they can make sense of what they may be sensing. The *worrying* (overly emotional, sizing) and *intruding* (myth of the smooth road) blind spots can interfere.

Honoring sovereignty:

> ► "Of course you're frightened, that makes sense after learning about this."
> ► "Those kinds of things hardly ever happen, and I feel safe here."
> ► "Change is hard and not usually fun, but it's a normal part of life."

Protecting the connection:

> ► "I feel sad, too. Let's learn more about this and see if we can help in some way."
> ► "Maybe we can take our feelings and let them lead us to do volunteer work together."
> ► "We're hurting a lot because of how much we care."

Presenting our lives as models:

> ► We can talk about this in a way that conveys our gratitude that the calamities are so rare.
> ► Model perspective by still going to school and work, walking the dog, and making the bed.
> ► Use fractions to explain—as in "100,000,000 people had ordinary days today, and one person did not. The ordinary days don't make it to the news."

MOMENT	Separation anxiety, cries at daycare or with babysitter.
LONG-TERM GOAL	Interpersonal skills: Boundaries and self-advocacy

They love us and they miss us. If the *worrying* blind spots (over-psychologizing), lead us to feel so upset or to wonder what the crying means we might have trouble seeing this as an opportunity to teach about boundaries. We strengthen them by allowing them to be comforted by others and giving them practice being away from us so they can learn to feel comfortable when they are.

Honoring sovereignty:
> "I understand you're sad, but I know you'll be fine."
> "It's important for you to learn how to be comfortable with babysitters, and Mommy and Daddy need time to go on dates once in a while."

Protecting the connection:
> We do not get frustrated, we do not get mad, and we do not give in either.
> "It's up to you whether you have fun or not. I can't crawl inside of you and make you happy."

Presenting our lives as models:
> The only times this kind of preschool challenge becomes a problem later is when the parents model that they too are upset and fail to stay strong when the crying starts.

MOMENT	A peer takes something that belongs to your child, gets in front of them in line.
LONG-TERM GOAL	Interpersonal skills: Boundaries and self-advocacy

While it is hard to see when our children are little, the ability to speak their minds and stand up for themselves will become critical when they are teenagers. All chances to teach assertiveness and self-advocacy skills are appreciated. The *worrying* (low tolerance for conflict, sizing) and *intruding* (over-help) blind spots can interfere.

Honoring sovereignty:

> ➤ "You were bothered today when this happened. How would you like to handle it next time?"
> ➤ "This is a normal part of childhood. Let's see what we can learn from it."

Protecting the connection:

> ➤ Sometimes children have to have permission by their parents in order to stand up for themselves.
> ➤ Without this permission, they might feel unsure about whether they are allowed to use a big voice or a firm tone or an angry look in their eyes.

Presenting our lives as models:

> ➤ "Let's role model: You pretend you're the other kid, and I'll be you. I'll show you how to handle this when it happens again."
> ➤ They will also be watching us when we deal with adults who get in front of us in line.

KINDERGARTEN–SECOND GRADE MISTAKES AND LONG-TERM GOALS

Kindergarten–Second Grade Mistakes	Long-term Goal: Emotional Calibration
Afraid to try new things. Refuses to go to school, says "I hate school," call from nurse's office. Comparing to others.	Thoughts precede feelings

Kindergarten–Second Grade Mistakes	Long-term Goal: Interpersonal Skills
Last minute refusal to go to a birthday party the child was looking forward to.	Boundaries and self-advocacy
Tattling, cry baby.	Boundaries and self-advocacy
Does not play well with a friend, mean to pets, saying unkind things.	Compassion
Lying, manipulates one parent against the other, says the teacher lied, lost their homework or picks on them.	That trust is important
Whiny, demanding, rude, talks back, moody, irritable, bossy, obnoxious, torments younger siblings, complaining, moping. Bossy with friends, takes things from other kids at school.	Personal growth process
Crying jags. Demands parent's undivided attention.	Stress management

Kindergarten–Second Grade Mistakes	Long-term Goal: Connected with Us
Says "No, you can't make me." Refuses to eat during mealtimes and then complains of being hungry between meals. Dawdles in the morning.	Perceive us accurately as their reservoir of confidence
Loses glasses, other expensive things. Acts like a spoiled child: "Get that for me, I want it."	Logical consequences by loving and forgiving parents

Kindergarten–Second Grade Mistakes	Long-term Goal: Work Ethic
Difficult mornings, hard to separate.	Defer gratification and develop patience
Chores, responsibilities, tidiness, procrastination, task completion.	Cooperate with authority
Missing assignments, says they will do something but then does not.	Importance of education
Put toys away, bed does not get made.	Defer gratification and develop patience

The format changes slightly now. In the preschool section, communication strategies were provided with the discussion of each moment and long-term goal. Now that the children are older, the communication strategies are placed at the end of each section. If you have not yet read the preschool section, I encourage you to do so even if your youngest child is already in school, because there are many examples that are also helpful with older children. In addition, please remember to refer back to Chapter 4 (Blind Spots), especially the sections labeled "Does this blind spot affect you," and "What to do about it."

MOMENT	Afraid to try new things. Refuses to go to school, says "I hate school," call from nurse's office. Comparing to others.
LONG-TERM GOAL	Emotional calibration: Thoughts precede feelings

Our 5- 6- and 7-year-olds can be nervous and have feelings of inadequacy. They can be hesitant to take on new challenges or feel frightened and lonely during the school day. When they look around to their peers, they can compare themselves to the others and wonder if they are good enough. If we focus only on their feelings and not also on their thoughts, we may not know how to help them. (Blind spots: overly emotional, over-psychologizing, poor listener, myth of the smooth road)

MOMENT	Last minute refusal to go to a birthday party the child was looking forward to.
LONG-TERM GOAL	Interpersonal skills: Boundaries and self-advocacy

Many parents are puzzled about how to handle children choosing not to go to some event that they had been looking forward to attending. Often we know that if we could get them there, they would have a great time, but it is rarely worth taking an adversarial position. Instead of cajoling and pressuring (because we know best) it is almost always better to teach about boundaries. They have the right to miss out on some fun, and we support their decision. If they regret their decision later that might be a great learning experience. (Blind spots: over-psychologizing, projecting linearly, cloning)

MOMENT	Tattling, cry baby.
LONG-TERM GOAL	Interpersonal skills: Boundaries and self-advocacy

Children this age get two different messages from parents and teachers: "Tell us if someone hurts you in any way," and "take care of things yourself." It makes perfect sense that they would be confused and perhaps tell us about every little thing during their first few years of school. We clarify that it is the big things we really want to hear about and the ordinary (non-traumatic) day-to-day incidents with other children we expect them to deal with as best they can. Then, when they bring a small matter to us, we can use it to teach them the skills they need to take care of themselves, rather than demean them by rescuing. (Blind spots: sizing, over-helping)

MOMENT	Does not play well with a friend, mean to pets, saying unkind things.
LONG-TERM GOAL	Interpersonal skills: Compassion

First- and 2nd-graders can be sensitive and compassionate one minute, and self-centered and unkind the next. This very typical problem can be observed without reacting. They are allowed to have this problem at this time. We look for a way to use this and begin talking about how the other child might feel, or how they would feel if someone treated them this way. As long as we do not get angry or impatient, they will be fine. (Blind spots: rulebooks, inserting intent)

MOMENT	Lying, manipulates one parent against the other, says the teacher lied, lost their homework or picks on them.
LONG-TERM GOAL	Interpersonal skills: That trust is important

Lying and manipulating can be viewed as serious problems or as harmless and cute, but they are almost an inevitable rite of passage for children. This is how they learn about trust. Viewed in this way, our approach is clear: We let them know that this is a problem for us, it goes against our family values and is something they need to work on. As long as we show up, represent our values and follow through with a consequence, this too shall pass. (Blind spots: lacks confidence, naïve, inserting intent)

MOMENT	Whiny, demanding, rude, talks back, moody, irritable, bossy, obnoxious, torments younger siblings, complaining, moping. Bossy with friends, takes things from other kids at school.
LONG-TERM GOAL	Interpersonal skills: Personal growth process

At this age, children can handle themselves so inappropriately that it is understandable that many parents find themselves losing their patience and their temper. But we already have one problem—we do not want to handle it in a way that creates a second problem! By our model, we show them their future. We want them to be able to handle stress, and we can show them how we handle stress when they are our stress. We use a calm voice, treat them better than they are treating us and discipline with reassurance. The pace of change is slow but will not be any faster if we get frustrated. (Blind spots: low tolerance for conflict, projecting linearly, rulebook)

MOMENT	Crying jags. Demands parent's undivided attention.
LONG-TERM GOAL	Interpersonal skills: Stress management

This type of moment is complicated because it seems more like neediness than a mistake. While there might be exceptional circumstances, very often the best strategy is to teach skills that build on their emerging autonomy to deal with stress themselves. As long as we do not do anything that inadvertently weakens them rather than strengthening them, this upsetting moment can be turned into a great teaching opportunity. (Blind spots: over-psychologizing, over-helping)

MOMENT	Says "No, you can't make me." Refuses to eat during mealtimes and then complains of being hungry between meals. Dawdles in the morning.
LONG-TERM GOAL	Connected to us: Perceive us accurately as their reservoir of confidence

When we observe this behavior without reacting (knowing many children make these mistakes), we can model calmness at times of stress. We can also handle it in a way that both addresses the need for a consequence and deepens their connection to us by our kind and loving tone. (Blind spots: rulebook, expect payback)

MOMENT	Loses glasses, other expensive things. Acts like a spoiled child: "Get that for me, I want it."
LONG-TERM GOAL	Connected to us: Logical consequences by loving and forgiving parents

It is not our favorite thing to have to replace expensive, lost items, but most children in the early grades will lose or break things. And sooner or later they will do an excellent impersonation of the world's most spoiled child! If we can see this as a chance to show up, give a consequence, forgive them and move on, we will have truly turned "lemons into lemonade." (Blind spots: projecting linearly, worships, naïve)

MOMENT	Difficult mornings, hard to separate.
LONG-TERM GOAL	Work ethic: Defer gratification and develop patience

With 6- and 7-year-olds, we can begin to use the difficult mornings to teach skills they will need to develop a successful work ethic. By viewing these kinds of moments as opportunities to teach about not always getting what they want and not always doing what they want to do, we can talk about patience and deferring gratification. (Blind spots: low tolerance for conflict, lacks confidence)

MOMENT	Chores, responsibilities, tidiness, procrastination, task completion.
LONG-TERM GOAL	Work ethic: Cooperate with authority

It is by struggling with their chores and responsibilities that they learn to cooperate with authority, now and in the future. Instead of getting frustrated, we can feel confident that they will be fine as long as we give them a consequence and do not make things worse by our reaction. (Blind spots: insert intent, lacks confidence)

MOMENT	Missing assignments, says they will do something but then does not.
LONG-TERM GOAL	Work ethic: Importance of education

Teaching the importance of education begins in the early grades but does not always seem to sink in until much later. Fortunately we can help them learn this by connecting their school work with things that are already important to them (like friends, teams, and screens). As long as we do not make things worse by our judging (rulebooks) or by our worrying (over-psychologizing, projecting linearly) blind spots, things will get better.

MOMENT	Put toys away, bed does not get made.
LONG-TERM GOAL	Work ethic: Defer gratification and develop patience

Parents often struggle needlessly with these everyday moments. It helps to remember that we do not actually have to get them to put their toys away or make their bed, we just have to follow through with a consequence if they do not. Time is on our side. Either way they grow. (Blind spots: rulebook, worships)

COMMUNICATION STRATEGIES

Honoring sovereignty:

- "Everybody is working on something—this is what you need to work on."
- "Lots of kids your age make this kind of mistake" in a forgiving tone.
- "You are really stuck here, aren't you sweetheart?"
- Remember: They are being the best 1st-graders that they can be at this time.
- Keeping in mind that kids this age do this, but it sure is stressful.
- Realizing that they are going to be their age the entire year.

Disciplining with reassurance:

- "You are having trouble with this, so you will lose this freedom until you improve."
- "This is hard for you. That's why we have to talk about it so much."
- "That kind of language is not acceptable. Here's your consequence."

Protecting the connection:

- "I guess we'll be talking about this a lot."
- "There is no rewind button in life, but we can do it differently next time."
- "This seems like one of those things I'm going to be saying a lot for now."
- Do not lose faith in the original strategy just because the mistake re-occurs.
- "I'm looking forward to this part of our journey together being over, sweetie."
- Humor: "I can't wait until they are done with this stage."
- As long as I do not add any fuel to their smoldering fire, we will be OK.

Presenting our lives as models:

- ➤ Our presence conveys that they are perfectly acceptable at the time of their mistake.
- ➤ Mistakes are a normal part of life. That is how children learn.
- ➤ "That hurts my ears. Please talk to me in your indoor voice."
- ➤ At least it is not (fill in the blank—something else more horrible)
- ➤ Humor: "Why should I be the only parent in town with a 2nd-grader who is nice to siblings!"

KINDERGARTEN–SECOND GRADE DISAPPOINTMENTS AND LONG-TERM GOALS

Kindergarten–Second Grade Disappointments	Long-term Goal: Resilience
Overheard an argument between parents.	What worth is based on
Trouble making or keeping friends.	Anticipate disappointments

Kindergarten–Second Grade Disappointments	Long-term Goal: Emotional Calibration
Grandparent (or friend's parent) is ill or dies. Friend's parents get divorced.	Language of feelings
Separation problems, gets upset when it is time to leave a friend's house. Bedtime worries.	Closure
Negative thinking. "Nobody likes me." "I'm no good in anything."	Optimism
Friend moves away, when a friend's parent dies at a young age.	Change and loss
Birthday party invitation does not come.	Sizing

Kindergarten–Second Grade Disappointments	Long-term Goal: Interpersonal Skills
Does not feel comfortable in bed at night, wants to be with parent. Transitions are hard, problems sharing and taking turns.	Boundaries and self-advocacy
Does not seem interested in play dates.	Internal locus of control

Kindergarten–Second Grade Disappointments	Long-term Goal: Work Ethic
Has a teacher who is more business-like than overly nurturing.	Ability to work with anyone

MOMENT   Overheard an argument between parents.

LONG-TERM GOAL   Resilience: What worth is based on

Even though we try to keep certain conversations private, sooner or later our children will hear something that upsets them. While the urge to immediately reassure them comes from love, this might provide an opportunity to acknowledge that relationships (including marriages) are hard work and require a lot of sharing about feelings. Sometimes people who love each other feel frustrated and express that in less than perfect ways. As adults, we know that our worth as a person, and the value of our marriage, does not hinge on every single conversation we have with our spouse, and children can be reassured by learning that their parents love each other and are continuing the conversation until they work things out. (Blind spots: overly emotional, low tolerance for conflict, over-psychologizing)

MOMENT   Trouble making or keeping friends.

LONG-TERM GOAL   Resilience: Anticipate disappointments

There are helpful resources in most libraries and bookstores for parents who sense that their children need help to develop their friendship skills. In addition, we can talk honestly with our children at this age about how life includes good times and bad times, friendships that last a long time and friendships that end. By normalizing this inevitable part of life, we can use this moment to strengthen them and prepare them for future disappointments. (Blind spots: overly emotional, myth of the smooth road, over-help)

MOMENT   Grandparent (or friend's parent) is ill or dies. Friend's parents get divorced.

LONG-TERM GOAL   Emotional calibration: Language of feelings

Children are more likely to benefit from rather than be harmed by accurate information. And it can be helpful to allow them to move through the stages of dealing with a difficult situation along with parents. When you are just hearing about Grandpa, tell your children then, not two weeks later. They will need to have the communication skills and the courage to talk about feelings their whole lives. (Blind spots: overly emotional, myth of smooth road)

MOMENT	Separation problems, gets upset when it is time to leave a friend's house. Bedtime worries.
LONG-TERM GOAL	Emotional calibration: Closure

If we just want to make them feel better or stop them from whining, we might miss a chance to teach about closure. First- and 2nd-graders can be encouraged to think about their day as it is, instead of comparing it to how they wished it could be. Time to say "goodbye" to us is time to say goodbye. Time to leave the friend's house is just that. If they get too upset, it is probably because they are thinking about in a way that causes them stress. We can model closure, as well as teach about it, by saying that after a few minutes it is time to do something else, talk about something else or at least let them know that you are done listening to it for now. (Blind spots: over-psychologizing, sizing)

MOMENT	Negative thinking. "Nobody likes me." "I'm no good in anything."
LONG-TERM GOAL	Emotional calibration: Optimism

The tendency to lunge in with cheerful platitudes is understandable but not usually helpful. Sooner or later all children struggle with feelings of doubt about their abilities, their friendships and their worth in general. The best strategy is to help them identify their options in how to think about their life and circumstances. Optimism is a learned trait, and it is almost impossible for them to learn it when they are comfortable and feeling great about themselves. It might

sound a little harsh, but it helps children if their parents say something like: "It makes sense that you would feel bad if you have to have
everyone in the world like you in order to feel good." (Blind spots:
overly emotional, sizing, projecting linearly)

MOMENT	Friend moves away, when a friend's parent dies at a young age.
LONG-TERM GOAL	Emotional calibration: Change and loss

As above, try to resist the urge to "tidy up" when events are not
tidy. Perfectly normal and healthy children will feel sad and frightened at these times. This is a time for us to teach about change and
loss, how much it helps to talk about our feelings, and coping plans
that include activity and diversion as well. The goal of parenting is not
to make sure they do not feel bad. It is to be connected to them in a
helpful way while they do. (Blind spots: over-psychologizing, poor
listener)

MOMENT	Birthday party invitation does not come.
LONG-TERM GOAL	Emotional calibration: Sizing

Please do not call the other parent and see if they have room for
one more child! It is a normal part of childhood to feel left out and
discouraged from time to time. Remind your children that they did
not invite the entire world to their birthday party either. You could
offer, "Maybe the parents only allowed six children to be invited and
you were seventh on the list." It is easy to teach this long-term goal
as long as the blind spot of the same name does not interfere. (Blind
spot: sizing)

> **MOMENT** Does not feel comfortable in bed at night, wants to be with parent. Transitions are hard, problems sharing and taking turns.
>
> **LONG-TERM GOAL** Interpersonal skills: Boundaries and self-advocacy

Many children miss their parents during the day and wish they could have more time with them before saying "goodnight." Some will discover that one way to obtain more time is by falling apart at bedtime. Other children continue to get upset easily during transitions or when they are with their friends. While it can be pleasant to spend a few extra minutes with them at bedtime, rubbing their back or reading an extra story, we also want to send them the message that we know they can learn how to comfort themselves. If we take on the problem as our own, it might get worse rather than better. And we remind them about sharing and taking turns, but we also give them accurate feedback about what we saw and how it might have been for their friend. (Blind spots: over-psychologizing, over-helping)

> **MOMENT** Does not seem interested in play dates.
>
> **LONG-TERM GOAL** Interpersonal skills: Internal locus of control

Most children love it when they can go over to a friend's house for a play date. But not all. If your child is one of those, remember to start where they are at and not compare them to how other children are. We want to honor our children's uniqueness even if we are puzzled. Some children are more introverted than others, worn out by the school week, or need more time alone to get themselves recharged. There is nothing unhealthy about being an introvert, but it worries parents anyway, especially if the parents are extroverts. (Blind spots: projecting linearly, rulebooks, cloning)

MOMENT Has a teacher who is more business-like than overly nurturing.

LONG-TERM GOAL Work ethic: Ability to work with anyone

Many great teachers in the early grades are warm and nurturing, but some of the good ones "run a tight ship" and are more business-like than lovey-dovey. While second grade might seem a bit young to help your children learn that it is up to them to adjust to their world (rather than expect the world to adjust to them), it is not too young. They will have all kinds of teachers, coaches, and bosses, and the ability to cooperate with appropriate authority figures will always be important. (Blind spots: overly emotional, worships)

COMMUNICATION STRATEGIES

Honoring sovereignty:

> ➤ "I have confidence that you will learn something good from this."
> ➤ "Let's see what this can teach us."
> ➤ "When you're done with this, we start working on the next issue because that is life."

Protecting the connection:

> ➤ "How can you handle this kind of thing if it happens tomorrow?"
> ➤ "How was the rest of your day?"
> ➤ "What could you *do* to change how you feel?"
> ➤ "How would you handle this if you had it to do again?"

Presenting our lives as models:

> ➤ Teach optimism: "You'll make friends someday—we just don't know when."
> ➤ Use famous sayings or proverbs. For example: "If a light is shining and no one can see it, is it still shining?" Explain that their inner beauty is like a shining light, and whether or not others see it, it is always there.
> ➤ "You come from tough stock. You can handle this, I know you can."
> ➤ "No law says all friendships last forever."
> ➤ "In our family, we try not to spend too much time feeling sorry for ourselves."

THIRD–FIFTH GRADE MISTAKES AND LONG-TERM GOALS

Third–Fifth Grade Mistakes	Long-term Goal: Resilience
Say they did not do it (when they did). Homework takes too long, gets down on self easily. Take something that does not belong to them, lose/break something. Temper outbursts.	What worth is based on

Third–Fifth Grade Mistakes	Long-term Goal: Emotional Calibration
Shows no remorse. Intense thinkers, worried and anxious often about many things.	Language of feelings
Often anxious, asks same question repeatedly, needs a lot of reassurance.	Closure
Raises voice, loses temper, slams door, "Not fair." Favoritism, being negative.	Thoughts precede feelings

Third–Fifth Grade Mistakes	Long-term Goal: Interpersonal Skills
When they are annoyed with us, complain about what horrible parents we are.	Communication and conflict resolution skills
Watches a "bad" show at a friend's house, cheats on a test, swears on the school bus.	That trust is important
Cannot play well alone, clingy, tries too hard to make friends, the other children do not like that.	The personal growth process

Third–Fifth Grade Mistakes	Long-term Goal: Connected to Us
Slams doors, without reminders they do nothing, but they complain about our nagging. Overly competitive or a poor sport/loser/gloating winner, steals something from a store.	Perceive us accurately as their reservoir of confidence
Talks back, rude to us, rolls their eyes, disrespectful to parents, ignores us. Inappropriate humor (bathroom jokes). Says something is done so they can do something, lies to cover up something.	Logical consequences by loving and forgiving parents

Third–Fifth Grade Mistakes	Long-term Goal: Work Ethic
Teacher calls. Report cards are mixed and include "could do better." Sunday night homework surprise. Unacceptable behavior lingers.	Importance of education
Gets frustrated and hits someone, steals, hides food in room, eats junk and lies about it, inappropriate use of hands.	Defer gratification and develop patience

Note: If you have not yet read the preschool section, I encourage you to do so even if your youngest child is already in 3rd grade, because there are many examples that are also helpful with older children. In addition, please remember to refer back to Chapter 4 (Blind Spots), especially the sections labeled "Does this blind spot affect you," and "What to do about it."

MOMENT	Say they did not do it (when they did). Homework takes too long, gets down on self easily. Take something that does not belong to them, loses or breaks something. Temper outbursts.
LONG-TERM GOAL	Resilience: What worth is based on

By the time our children are in third grade, it becomes pretty easy to discipline with reassurance at times of mistakes. The harder part seems to be staying patient and remembering that they will not change faster if we handle our part poorly. Even though "getting down on themselves" has a different feel to it, we can still view it as a mistake. But we can teach that their worth does not require a mistake-free life or a struggle-free life. While we are saying our words of encouragement (or explaining their consequence), we clarify the difference between the ups and downs of childhood and what their worth is based on. (Blind spots: rulebooks, sizing)

MOMENT	Shows no remorse. Intense thinkers, worried and anxious often about many things.
LONG-TERM GOAL	Emotional calibration: Language of feelings

Children sometimes are reluctant to admit they did something wrong. When adults have this problem, it looks like a serious problem (does not take responsibility, shows no remorse), but it is not usually serious at this age. Instead, view it as an opportunity to model forgiveness and to teach how much better it feels to face up to a mistake, take your medicine and move on. Some children benefit from smaller consequences at such times. Similarly, there may be no better time to teach about the language of feelings than when they are worried and anxious. (Blind spots: insert intent, over-psychologizing)

MOMENT	Often anxious, asks same question repeatedly, needs a lot of reassurance.
LONG-TERM GOAL	Emotional calibration: Closure

What can seem like something is very wrong—following us from room to room, not wanting to be alone upstairs, needing a lot of reassurance—can be nothing more than a skill deficit about closure. Children this age often feel ruled by their feelings and they need help from us to teach and model how to think about things to keep them small and feel done with them. (Blind spots: overly emotional, sizing, over-help)

MOMENT	Raises voice, loses temper, slams door, "Not fair." Favoritism, being negative.
LONG-TERM GOAL	Emotional calibration: Thoughts precede feelings

All children lose their temper and whine about favoritism. It helps us know how to proceed when we view this as a sign that our children are thinking about their moments in a way that makes them feel "too much something." At times, their thoughts lead them to feel too angry, too frustrated, left out, or unfairly treated, and at those times we can help them identify the thoughts and begin the lifetime work of changing how they feel by changing what they think. (Blind spots: rulebooks, projecting linearly)

MOMENT	When they are annoyed with us, complain about what horrible parents we are.
LONG-TERM GOAL	Interpersonal skills: Communication and conflict resolution skills

This also is an inevitable part of parenting 3rd- 4th- and 5th-graders. By listening without getting defensive and resisting the urge to argue with them or remind them how good they have it, we can focus instead on demonstrating our excellent communication and conflict resolution skills. We model for them how we expect them to handle these situations when they are older. (Blind spots: overly emotional, low tolerance for conflict)

MOMENT	Watches a "bad" show at a friend's house, cheats on a test, swears on the school bus.
LONG-TERM GOAL	Interpersonal skills: That trust is important

The world begins to impose on the bubble we wish we could keep our children in, and how we respond is more critical than their mistake. We have to parent expecting our children to learn "naughty" words, swear, cheat and make other nerve-wracking mistakes as well. Disciplining with reassurance and modeling forgiveness will address the present situation and protect the connection for the future at the same time. (Blind spots: rulebooks, projecting linearly)

MOMENT	Cannot play well alone, clingy, tries too hard to make friends and the other children do not like that.
LONG-TERM GOAL	Interpersonal skills: The personal growth process

If we could prevent our children from ever being uncomfortable, we would. Instead we teach them how to grow. What skills could be lacking that could perhaps best be learned at this time? We do not solve these problems for our children. We help them view them honestly and begin a personal growth process. (Blind spots: sizing, poor listener, over-help)

MOMENT	Slams doors, without reminders they do nothing, but they complain about our nagging. Overly competitive or a poor sport/loser/gloating winner, steals something from a store.
LONG-TERM GOAL	Connected to us: Perceive us accurately as their reservoir of confidence

It is almost as if they set a trap for us, baiting us with their behavior so that we respond in a way that makes things worse. Even these moments can be regarded simply as mistakes and opportunities to teach. Yes, consequences are helpful. And sometimes the pace of change is slow. But perhaps the most important long-term goal at this age from such behaviors is for our children to sense our confidence in them and the certainty that our love for them is unchanged at times of mistakes. (Blind spots: rulebooks, expect payback, lacks confidence)

MOMENT	Talks back, rude to us, rolls their eyes, disrespectful to parents, ignores us. Inappropriate humor (bathroom jokes). Says something is done so they can do something, lies to cover up something.
LONG-TERM GOAL	Connected to us: Logical consequences by loving and forgiving parents

It is worth repeating: logical consequences by loving and forgiving parents are enough. Sometimes when we want to control them, the best strategy is controlling ourselves. Talking to parents of teenagers can provide a perspective that helps us be the best "us" we can be at all times, including times when we feel worn out and begin to wonder whether they will ever stop driving us crazy. (Blind spots: overly emotional, low tolerance for conflict)

MOMENT	Teacher calls. Report cards are mixed and include "could do better." Sunday night homework surprise. Unacceptable behavior lingers.
LONG-TERM GOAL	Work ethic: Importance of education

Before fourth grade, it makes sense for us to help as much as we can (look in their backpack, be their organizational system, get them started with their homework, sit with them if needed). But it is important for us to begin turning over the responsibility for their school career to them at some point in time. Children seem to learn the importance of education more easily during fourth and fifth grade if their parents take a half step back and allow them the dignity of being in charge. Even if things get worse for a short period of time and we need to connect their school performance with privileges or consequences, the overall process leads to an internalization of the skills needed for success in later years. (Blind spots: projecting linearly, expect payback, over-help)

MOMENT	Gets frustrated and hits someone, steals, hides food in room, eats junk and lies about it, inappropriate use of hands.
LONG-TERM GOAL	Work ethic: Defer gratification and develop patience

There are few skills more important to success than self-control and there is no easier time to develop these skills than when they are absent. The trap for parents seems to be responding with their own poor impulse control when their children lie, hit, steal or hide food in their room. Be careful about modeling that children have to have self-control, but parents do not. (Blind spots: overly emotional, sizing)

COMMUNICATION STRATEGIES

Honoring sovereignty

➤ "You've been having trouble controlling your temper lately. I have some ideas on how you can improve."

➤ "It's not my favorite thing when you act like this, but I know that a lot of children your age do make these kinds of mistakes from time to time."

➤ "Your father and I know you can do better in school, and we are concerned that you don't realize yet how important it is to get a good education. We think you might be too busy and too distracted with so many other activities."

Protecting the connection

➤ "One way we are going to help you do better in school is by taking you off the team and not allowing you to see friends on weekends until you show us that you are taking school more seriously."

➤ "If you scream at me and run down the hall and slam the door, I will have to give you a consequence. But that is all that happens. I won't go running down the hall after you, and I won't scream at you to get you to stop screaming at me."

➤ "I guess every child your age goes to a secret school somewhere to learn how to roll their eyes like that in order to drive their parents crazy! It won't work with me, sweetie. I'm your biggest fan."

➤ "It would be easier if you could just admit to your mistake, take your consequence and let us move on. But this is still hard for you, so I'll help you with it until you figure it out."

➤ "I wish you hadn't watched that particular show, but I'm glad I found out about it. This way I can help you understand what you saw and tell you what our family believes and how our family does things."

Presenting our lives as models

> ➤ They are allowed to act like a 10-year-old; we are not. There is a higher standard of behavior for us.
> ➤ As long as we do not race them to the basement and mirror them when they are at their worst, we will not have to worry very much about the future.
> ➤ There are teaching opportunities in every tantrum, every self-absorbed moment, and every time the teacher calls with bad news.
> ➤ As long as we are in control of ourselves, our children will learn to be in control of themselves as soon as they possibly can.

THIRD–FIFTH GRADE DISAPPOINTMENTS AND LONG-TERM GOALS

Third–Fifth Grade Disappointments	Long-term Goals: Resilience
Misses out on something fun the other kids are doing. Challenges with friendships, changes in status in the peer hierarchy.	Self-esteem is not contingent on a smooth road
Disciplined by teacher in front of peers. Experiences discrimination.	Anticipate disappointments

Third–Fifth Grade Disappointments	Long-term Goals: Emotional Calibration
They begin to notice that certain academic subjects are harder for them than for other students.	Optimism
Seems afraid to do overnights.	Thoughts precede feelings
Plays poorly, team loses because of something they did.	Sizing

Third–Fifth Grade Disappointments	Long-term Goals: Interpersonal Skills
Excluded, no one to play with at recess, being teased.	Communication and conflict resolution skills
Does not make the team or the talent show.	Boundaries and self-advocacy
Early examples of peer pressure and wanting to be accepted.	Boundaries and self-advocacy

Third–Fifth Grade Disappointments	Long-term Goals: Work Ethic
Friend has an untraditional family structure.	Ability to work with anyone

MOMENT	Misses out on something fun the other kids are doing. Challenges with friendships, changes in status in the peer hierarchy.
LONG-TERM GOAL	Resilience: Self-esteem is not contingent on a smooth road

The disappointments are still pretty small, and with help, children learn to view them this way. The best strategy is to normalize the missed opportunity as a perfectly reasonable part of life. (Did they think they would be able to do everything they wanted to do?) Friendship issues are paramount at these ages, and they provide great opportunities to teach that belonging is dessert, not the main course. Some teenagers who make unfortunate decisions during high school do so because they are trying too hard to fit in or be accepted by their peers. The ones who seem more capable of resisting this trap are the ones who learned years earlier how to feel comfortable with themselves even when they do not belong to a popular crowd. (Blind spots: overly emotional, sizing, cloning)

MOMENT	Disciplined by teacher in front of peers. Experiences discrimination.
LONG-TERM GOAL	Resilience: Anticipate disappointments

Rather than mirroring our children's emotional reactions (getting very upset ourselves, retaliating against the teacher or the person who discriminated), we can model that we are more experienced than they are at living in this imperfect world of ours. Things happen but they do not have to cause us to feel any certain way. In fact, we teach how to respond when others make mistakes. When we remember that our children become resilient by watching us at stressful times, we know how to proceed. (Blind spots: myth of smooth road, worships children)

MOMENT	They begin to notice that certain academic subjects are harder for them than for other students.
LONG-TERM GOAL	Emotional calibration: Optimism

An optimistic outlook is important for all children, but perhaps most important for those who struggle with something like academics. Parents want to be able to model (every day—including report card day) that we do not equate being good at math with being a good person. Optimistic children view difficult challenges as difficult challenges, not as a measure of their worth. (Blind spots: overly emotional, myth of smooth road, over-help)

MOMENT	Seems afraid to do overnights.
LONG-TERM GOAL	Emotional calibration: Thoughts precede feelings

There are two different parts to this. First, overnights are not an essential part of childhood, and this can be an opportunity to model how we are not comparing children to how others are or how they should be. The second part requires us to observe without reacting, and through our connection with our children, learn to see this through their eyes. What are their thoughts that precede their fear about overnights? Can we help them modify those thoughts, and by doing so, teach them how to feel differently? Blind spots: (over-psychologizing, poor listener)

MOMENT	Plays poorly, team loses because of something they did.
LONG-TERM GOAL	Emotional calibration: Sizing

It makes perfect sense to us that 4th- and 5th-graders would get upset when they feel responsible for a loss and their teammates are annoyed. The best way to celebrate this kind of a disappointment is by remembering that these are the times that permit children to learn about sizing. We do not feel (or look or act) traumatized. In fact, we point out that professional athletes strike out and drop touchdown passes. Their teammates are making their own mistake by how they are behaving, but that does not have to cause us to feel any certain way. (Blind spots: overly emotional, sizing, myth of the smooth road)

MOMENT	Excluded, no one to play with at recess, being teased.
LONG-TERM GOAL	Interpersonal skills: Communication and conflict resolution skills

Recess can be a lonely or hurtful time, and the urge to rescue is huge. If we keep our focus between us and our children (rather than between them and the playground), we can usually find the skill they need to learn or the tactic that will be most helpful. In years to come we will want them to be impervious to what their peers are doing and to know how to feel good during less-than-perfect times. Children benefit from doing role-plays with us: They act out what the others are doing, and we show them acceptable responses they can make. (Blind spots: overly emotional, projecting linearly, myth of the smooth road)

MOMENT	Does not make the team or the talent show.
LONG-TERM GOAL	Interpersonal skills: Boundaries and self-advocacy

Even though our children may seem very talented athletically or academically to us, there are actually a lot of talented children out there. Many children have in their future getting cut from a team, doing poorly on important tests or bumping into limits in some other way. The goal of parenting is not to get them into the talent show. Rather it is to teach them how to feel comfortable with what they get and with what they do not get. All of us have limits, and as children move towards greater independence and autonomy, we want to help them know that they will have a good enough, though imperfect life (just like the rest of us). (Blind spots: worships children, cloning, over-helps)

MOMENT	Early examples of peer pressure and wanting to be accepted.
LONG-TERM GOAL	Interpersonal skills: Boundaries and self-advocacy

Sooner or later children do something wrong and say they did it because their friend "made them do it." While it can be tempting to see it this way ourselves (and try to discourage this particular friendship), it is more helpful to view this as a signal that our children were susceptible to this peer influence. That keeps the focus between our children and us and directs our energies to teaching them how to stand up for themselves and stay true to their own sense of right and wrong. We also hold them 100 percent accountable for their actions. (Blind spots: over-psychologizing, naïve)

MOMENT	Friend has divorced parents, fathers with girl friends, mothers with boyfriends, a blended family or an untraditional family structure.
LONG-TERM GOAL	Work ethic: Ability to work with anyone

Some parents are unsure how to handle the many configurations family life can take. I hesitated to include this under "disappointments," but decided to because many children are confused and disappointed when they first discover the many variations of family life. Since their future will be in a world made up of many different people and relationships, it is better to talk plainly about what is, and to model your comfort and acceptance. People do not have to be any one way (or just like us) to be worthy and to be possible friends. (Blind spots: rulebooks, myth of smooth road)

COMMUNICATION STRATEGIES

Honoring sovereignty:

> ▸ "This is a confusing time for you, with many changes and new feelings."
>
> ▸ "Your friends are important to you, and it makes sense that you might feel worried sometimes about where you fit in."
>
> ▸ "Everybody takes turns missing out on fun activities like birthday parties. It's disappointing, but it doesn't mean there is anything wrong with you."
>
> ▸ "Try not to worry too much about this at bedtime. Things always seem more upsetting when it's dark outside. Let's set aside time tomorrow afternoon and talk about it when the sun is up. For now, let's read a favorite story."
>
> ▸ "If math continues to be hard for you, we'll get you some extra help. But, please remember, math is just one subject, and you are so much more to us than a math student!"
>
> ▸ "Even if it takes a bit longer for you to figure this new material out, that only means you'll need to give it more time. We are only comparing you to who you were yesterday, and we see progress every day. We're not comparing you to anybody else."

Protecting the connection:

> ▸ "We'll get through this together. That's my job, my pleasure, and what I do."
>
> ▸ "You are number one in my book. That's more important than whatever number you are in anyone else's book."
>
> ▸ "Even though your report card was a little disappointing to you, please remember that your mother and I evaluate you every single day, not only on report card day. And we really like what we've been seeing every day. You've been using your planner, you come home with everything you need, and you get to work. In time, the grades will improve."

Presenting our lives as models:

> ➤ They are watching us handle our stress, whether it is from work, in-laws, traffic or the stress that they cause us on a typical day.
> ➤ Sometimes we can look like giants to our children, or at least look as if we are always competent and successful. If we bring in examples of our day-to-day disappointments, we can show them that it is a normal part of life to have a colleague who gets more recognition that we do, to be scolded by a boss, or to miss out on a promotion.

SIXTH–EIGHTH GRADE MISTAKES AND LONG-TERM GOALS

Sixth–Eighth Grade Mistakes	Long-term Goals: Resilience
Inappropriate use of media, television, movies, computer games, internet, music.	Anticipate disappointments

Sixth–Eighth Grade Mistakes	Long-term Goals: Emotional Calibration
Does not open up, keeps feelings in.	Language of feelings
Too hard on self, everything is a big deal, perfectionistic.	Closure

Sixth–Eighth Grade Mistakes	Long-term Goals: Interpersonal Skills
Underachieving, attitude towards school.	Boundaries and self-advocacy
Power struggles and defiance, arguing about small matters.	Communication and conflict resolution skills
Speaking inappropriately about the other gender's developing bodies.	Compassion
Follows the lead of a friend (wrong crowd).	Internal locus of control

Sixth–Eighth Grade Mistakes	Long-term Goals: Connected to Us
Rude, seems like disrespect. Sees us as dumber than dirt, rolls their eyes at us, uses sarcasm.	Perceive us accurately as their reservoir of confidence

Chores done carelessly. Tries to manipulate us. Resists participation in family activities. Boys and pornography.	Logical consequences by loving and forgiving parents

Sixth–Eighth Grade Mistakes	Long-term Goals: Work Ethic
Time management, promptness, planning ahead, not using potential, poor grades. Says they do not have any homework in order to be able to do something. Not planning for the project that is due in two weeks.	Defer gratification and develop patience

Note: If you have not yet read the preschool section, I encourage you to do so even if your youngest child is already in 6th grade, because there are many examples that are also helpful with older children. In addition, please remember to refer back to Chapter 4 (Blind Spots), especially the sections labeled "Does this blind spot affect you," and "What to do about it."

MOMENT	Inappropriate use of media, television, movies, computer games, internet, music.
LONG-TERM GOAL	Resilience: Anticipate disappointments

It seems reasonable to keep screens to a minimum, especially on school nights. Many families provide (and then fight over) electronic games and cell phones. Keep computers in the public rooms of the house (not the bedrooms) and the games in a closet for use on weekends and road trips. Passwords and filters are helpful for the Internet and at the same time, we know that their future will include being exposed to "garbage" despite our best efforts. When children make mistakes that provide us openings to talk about what is out there in a realistic and unexcited way, it can take a mistake and turn it into a teaching opportunity. (Blind spots: overly emotional, lacks confidence)

MOMENT	Does not open up, keeps feelings in.
LONG-TERM GOAL	Emotional calibration: Language of feelings

Middle school children (perhaps the boys more than the girls) can clam up and become reluctant to share much about their feelings or even their day. Pouncing ("you sit right here and tell me what's going on") does not usually work very well. Sometimes they need ideal conditions to talk, and those might be hard to come by given the pace of family life. Creating the conditions is important. Families have volunteered together or used yard work or household projects as ways to increase the opportunities for sharing. Many children will not share at home with siblings around, dinner being made and phones ringing. It is not simply a matter of blaming them for not sharing. We have to be able to figure out what they need from us to learn the benefits of talking about their emotional lives. We all know adults who had trouble in their marriages because they did not learn the language of feelings when they were younger. It has always struck me as particularly unfortunate when 12- or 13-year-olds are all bottled up and their parents describe a frantic lifestyle, with children signed up for many activities. While unintentional, these families allowed themselves to become so busy that there was no time left for their children to develop this skill. (Blind spots: low tolerance for conflict, poor listener)

MOMENT	Too hard on self, everything is a big deal, perfectionistic.
LONG-TERM GOAL	Emotional calibration: Closure

Even though we try to teach closure to children when they are younger, adolescence seems to bring them back to a self-critical style. They are often not comfortable with their appearance, how many friends they have or how easy other children have it. Fortunately their cognitive abilities continue to develop, and they may be able to learn about the role thoughts play in feelings. We use our lives to model how we obtain closure: No matter how stressful the day, we are glad to come home and direct our thoughts to the pleasures all around us. Be careful about becoming so worried about grades that you inadvertently add fuel to the perfectionism. If they are already being hard on themselves, how will it help for them to perceive us as disappointed in them? It is always reasonable to connect their school performance with weekend opportunities, sports or music. It is never helpful to use interpersonal tension as a consequence. (Blind spots: overly emotional, sizing)

MOMENT	Underachieving, attitude towards school.
LONG-TERM GOAL	Interpersonal skills: Boundaries and self-advocacy

---

If children have not yet learned that they are the only ones responsible for their academic career, now is a good time. Instead of making things worse (by being mad and disappointed in them, being their organizer and planner), we can make things better by connecting their attitude and effort with the parts of life that matter the most to them. If you think it is hard to tolerate poor grades in sixth grade, please know that it is not nearly as hard as having someone like me tell you when your children are in ninth grade that this problem would have been resolved by now if you had only taught them about boundaries three years ago. They can only internalize the skills they need to be successful in school without the extra help, the extra interpersonal tension and without the confusion of having parents over-involved with their academic career. (Blind spots: expecting payback, cloning, over-help, worships)

MOMENT	Power struggles and defiance, arguing about small matters.
LONG-TERM GOAL	Interpersonal skills: Communication and conflict resolution skills

Eleven- and 12-year-olds are famous for reducing their parents to an 11- or 12-year-old pattern of behavior. If we are not careful, we race them to the basement: The more obnoxious they act the more critical and judgmental we are. But there is a higher standard for our behavior, we are the adults after all. They are the only ones with the right to act their age. By modeling our communication and conflict resolution skills, our children will in time come to resemble us. It may help to remember that they are supposed to engage us in power struggles as they work on developing their autonomy. The day-to-day arguments about trivial matters are an integral part of this process. We only have to worry if we respond poorly. When they are pushing us back and being difficult for no apparent reason, we can remember what the reason actually is (adolescence!) and use the moment to teach communication and conflict resolution skills. (Blind spots: rulebooks, expect payback, insert intent)

MOMENT	Speaking inappropriately about the other gender's developing bodies.
LONG-TERM GOAL	Interpersonal skills: Compassion

An unfortunate but apparently unavoidable rite of passage for teenagers is their preoccupation with the changing bodies around them, and most will speak in disrespectful ways about how someone looks or whether they are hot or not. While we would like to intervene to stop this once and for all, it is enough to discipline with reassurance and use this mistake to teach about compassion. After all, this is just the beginning of their journey with the opposite sex. They have many years of dating ahead of them and there is so much we want to teach them for that part of their journey. At least their inappropriate comments provide us with a perfect conversation starter. We can take the lesson in whatever direction we think they need, including their feelings of sexual arousal, the importance of respect or self-control. (Blind spots: overly emotional, projecting linearly, lacks confidence)

MOMENT	Follows the lead of a friend (wrong crowd).
LONG-TERM GOAL	Interpersonal skills: Internal locus of control

If children still want to be accepted by the wrong crowd at this age, we have every reason to be concerned. Some of their peers might be making very poor choices already. While we supervise and monitor and have our family rules, we engage in a tug of war: all that we represent and the connection we have been protecting all these years versus all that the peers represent. By now we hope they know to follow their inner voice and that their worth does not hinge on belonging to a popular group. It is relatively easy to lecture them about who they should choose for friends, but difficult to connect with them so that they value our guidance. (Blind spots: overly emotional, low tolerance for conflict, naïve)

MOMENT	Rude, seems like disrespect. Sees us as dumber than dirt, rolls their eyes at us, uses sarcasm.
LONG-TERM GOAL	Connected to us: Perceive us accurately as their reservoir of confidence

This one is included here because of the obvious irony. Just when we are engaged in this urgent tug of war with our children's peers, their behavior can wear us out and lead us to react to them in a way that strengthens the peers' influence. There they are, influenced by their friends and acting obnoxious and disrespectful like their friends, and we want to respond in a way that both disciplines and brings them closer to us as 12 becomes 13 and 14. (Blind spots: rulebooks, expecting payback, inserting intent)

MOMENT	Chores done carelessly. Tries to manipulate us. Resists participation in family activities. Boys and pornography.
LONG-TERM GOAL	Connected to us: Logical consequences by loving and forgiving parents

Disciplining with reassurance is enough for poorly done chores, for their attempts to manipulate us and even if they visit pornographic websites! Even this is a mistake (certainly a big one). However, while we are saying the obvious words about respect and exploitation, we are also protecting the connection. We want *all the boys* to talk to us about their thoughts and feelings while dating, not just the boys who never visited a pornographic website. If a parent explodes in anger about this frequently occurring but distasteful mistake, the boy may become less likely to share. We need to be able to teach that it is wrong while we reassure our sons that we understand their powerful feelings and how confusing things are for them at this time.

We also understand that they are less eager to go on family outings with us, especially if it involves their younger siblings. Some parents divide these family events into negotiable ones, like picnics, parks and beaches; and non-negotiable ones, like visiting grandparents and weddings. (Blind spots: overly emotional, sizing, rulebooks)

MOMENT	Time management, promptness, planning ahead, not using potential, poor grades. Says they do not have any homework in order to be able to do something. Not planning for the project that is due in two weeks.
LONG-TERM GOAL	Connected to us: Defer gratification and develop patience

Their school success is critical, and middle school feels late to still be struggling with time management and effort issues. But we can only start where they are at, and try not to judge. If they have not learned these skills yet, then they have not learned these skills yet. Instead of being furious with them, maybe it is partly our fault. In any case, we hold them accountable, connect achievement with the things that matter to them, and we do it all in a forgiving and loving manner. They need to feel solely responsible for their academic career and to know that there is no cavalry on its way. (Blind spots: over-helps, lacks confidence)

COMMUNICATION STRATEGIES

Honoring sovereignty:

> ▶ Accepting that they will be self-absorbed and challenging does not prevent us from staying true to our values and disciplining with reassurance. In fact, it is the only thing that will allow us to treat them with respect and dignity when that is not the way they are treating us.

> ▶ We can honor this transition to adolescence by remembering that we and all of our friends were 11, 12, or 13 at one time, and not only did we survive, but our parents survived as well.

> ▶ We do not need them to already have a fully developed appreciation for the importance of a good education. Very few children do at this age.

> ▶ Their years of growth and maturity will continue for several more years. Now, more than ever, it helps to view them as "works in progress."

Protecting the connection:

> ▶ By connecting what is important to us (their academic career), with what is important to them (participation in activities, certain freedoms, being able to see friends), we build bridges to a point in the future when they will intrinsically value education.

> ▶ Since we have this power, we never have to respond to an academic problem in a way that threatens the parent-child relationship.

> ▶ Middle school teachers know that the best way to help students cooperate and thrive is to convince them that they are valued, liked and forgiven.

> ▶ This is equally true at home. If your 12-year-old believes you have forgiven them the instant they act inappropriately, they are more likely to apologize, the incident is less likely to escalate, and they are better able to look in their own mirror and focus on the work they need to do.

Presenting our lives as models:

> Treating them the way we want them to treat us is a very powerful and effective parenting strategy for middle school students.
> It is calming and soothing for them to see us shrug our shoulders, shake our head, smile a small smile, instead of raising our voice and taking them on.
> Their sequencing skills are so poor, that if we are not careful, they will conclude that our reaction to their inappropriate behavior actually caused their inappropriate behavior.

SIXTH–EIGHTH GRADE DISAPPOINTMENTS AND LONG-TERM GOALS

Sixth–Eighth Grade Disappointments	Long-term Goals: Resilience
Not making a team, does not play much, needs extra help in reading or math.	What worth is based on
Rumors spread about your child. Accused unfairly.	Self-esteem is not contingent on a smooth road

Sixth–Eighth Grade Disappointments	Long-term Goals: Emotional Calibration
Closest friend (and family) moving out of the area.	Optimism
Mood swings, compares self to others, puts self down, life on the roller coaster.	Thoughts precede feelings
Friend stops being a friend and says or sends unkind comments, sobs after school.	Sizing

Sixth–Eighth Grade Disappointments	Long-term Goals: Interpersonal Skills
Conflict with teacher or coach.	Boundaries and self-advocacy
Expelled from a group of friends. Girls talking behind their backs.	That trust is important

MOMENT	Not making a team, does not play much, needs extra help in reading or math.
LONG-TERM GOAL	Resilience: What worth is based on

We continue to teach that their worth as a person is not based on their athletic or academic ability. We understand they may feel discouraged, but that is different from devastated. With our help they learn to be comfortable in their own skin without comparing themselves to others who are better than them in one area or another. This may be our greatest gift to our children, and in order to teach it, we must first believe it ourselves. We want them to be successful in whatever is important to them, but that is not in our power to arrange. We have to teach our children not only to use their talents well, but also to be comfortable with the talents they have and the talents they do not have. (Blind spots: cloning, myth of smooth road)

MOMENT	Rumors spread about your child. Accused unfairly.
LONG-TERM GOAL	Resilience: Self-esteem is not contingent on a smooth road

With the level of self-consciousness so high at this age, it hardly seems fair for rumors and gossip to be so prevalent. Here is where a lifetime of modeling that external events do not control how we feel begins to pay off. We teach that they have a choice in how they view the actions of others. Just because the other children say something does not make it true. The statements and actions of others only have power over us if we give our power away to them. We do not have to get the other children to stop what they are doing in order for us to help our children feel better. In fact, there may be no other time more perfectly suited for teaching our children how to think their way out of feeling hurt or lonely. We will know we are there when they say: "Who cares what they think? They don't know me and I don't need them to like me!" (Blind spots: overly emotional, poor listener)

MOMENT	Closest friend (and family) moving out of the area.
LONG-TERM GOAL	Emotional calibration: Optimism

While some children seem to have all the friends they need, others tend to only allow one or two in close. What happens if their closest friend has to move to another part of the country? Even though we cannot prevent our children from hurting, we can at least teach them strategies to minimize their pain. This will not be the last time in their lives that they will have to cope with an unwanted change or loss. Perhaps all we can do for them is to teach them how to view such moments. It is easier than ever to stay in touch, and family vacations can be arranged to allow visits. Hopefully, even if they feel sad, they do not feel devastated, and they believe that new friends are out there waiting to be found. (Blind spots: sizing, myth of smooth road)

MOMENT	Mood swings, compares self to others, puts self down, life on the roller coaster.
LONG-TERM GOAL	Emotional calibration: Thoughts precede feelings

These are going to be years of emotional swings. On their good days our children might see themselves as uniquely special, on their bad days, as so unworthy that they believe they deserve to be treated with scorn. Our role is not to cheer them up or grow impatient with them, but rather to be invited in, so we can see things through their eyes. How else will we be able to teach them about their options in how they view their life events? The trap here seems to be that merely cheering them up does not teach them anything that will be helpful to them in the future. It might even foster an unhealthy dependence on us as somehow responsible for making them feel better. (Blind spots: poor listener, over-helps)

MOMENT Friend stops being a friend and says or sends unkind comments, sobs after school.

LONG-TERM GOAL Emotional calibration: Sizing

Ideally children learn from the drama of 4th- and 5th-grade friendship issues how to view the unkind actions of others. However the physical and emotional changes of middle school require us to use every possible moment to teach about sizing. With our help, they can so effectively develop this skill, that no matter what their peers throw at them, they can successfully see it as small. (Blind spots: overly emotional, over-psychologizing)

MOMENT Conflict with teacher or coach.

LONG-TERM GOAL Interpersonal skills: Boundaries and self-advocacy

Sooner or later children have to deal with a difficult situation with a teacher or a coach, and we may feel an urge to rush in and take care of things. However, that strategy may be weakening rather than strengthening. They might even decide that you did not have the confidence in them to allow them to struggle with it themselves. We can role play with them at home, help them develop the skills they need, and send them out to represent themselves. (Blind spots: poor listener, over-helps)

MOMENT Expelled from a group of friends. Girls talking behind their backs.

LONG-TERM GOAL Interpersonal skills: That trust is important

Here again we would take away their emotional pain if we could, but is it not important for children to learn about loyalty and treachery? How else can children learn the wisdom of casting a wide net and not putting all of their dependency needs in one basket? We want to teach them that how they feel depends on something inside of them, not on changes the others make. (Blind spots: overly emotionally, cloning)

COMMUNICATION STRATEGIES

Honoring sovereignty:

> ➤ Adolescence is temporary, and what they are going through is only their present, not their future.
>
> ➤ They begin to need to hear reassurances from us that they will be fine even if they are not as successful in one area or another as they (or we) always hoped or assumed they would be.
>
> ➤ When disappointments occur, it is possible to convince 12- and 13-year-olds that they are "good enough" exactly the way they are, as long as we believe it ourselves.
>
> ➤ Be careful if it is hard for you to honor your children's genuine limitations. If they sense that you are disappointed in them, you may hurt them more than any report card or missed opportunity ever will.

Protecting the connection:

> ➤ "This doesn't define who you are as a person. This is just hockey (math, piano)."
>
> ➤ "If those ex-friends of yours can't see what a terrific kid you are, then they aren't worthy of you. To me, you are the best!"
>
> ➤ "Try not to let the rumors bother you too much. Those kids spreading them are allowed to make mistakes. In time, they'll look back on this with their own regrets."

Presenting our lives as models:

> ➤ Since this time of life is so stressful for our children, it is reasonable to assume that virtually all of their worst moments are due to the craziness of early adolescence.
>
> ➤ Believing this wholeheartedly will help you be the best "you" when they are impossible.
>
> ➤ They are always watching us, even when they are not listening.
>
> ➤ Show them how you hope they act in the (very near) future.

HIGH SCHOOL MISTAKES AND LONG-TERM GOALS

High School Mistakes	Long-term Goals: Emotional Calibration
Falling in love, thinks it is the "real thing."	Language of feelings
Copes with stress poorly, either by denial and avoidance, or by getting angry when anxious.	Thoughts precede feelings

High School Mistakes	Long-term Goals: Interpersonal Skills
Controlled or overly influenced by (or clingy and possessive with) boyfriend or girlfriend.	Boundaries and self-advocacy
Loud, boisterous, monopolizes conversations, rude, bad manners, shallow or self-centered.	Personal growth process
Steals money from a high school job. Drifting, seems aimless, no sense of direction.	Stress management

High School Mistakes	Long-term Goals: Connected to Us
Isolates in their room, one-word answers about their day. Not telling us about their plans for the evening. Not open to our guidance (apply for a job early enough, scholarships). Wants to work after high school instead of going to college.	Perceive us accurately as their reservoir of confidence

Disagrees with everything we say even before we say it, curfew violations. Decisions made about dating, drinking or drug use during high school. Full of themselves, no time for family, goes out a lot, aloof, indifferent to family. Pursues interest in something parent does not value. When they seem to have no use for us in their lives anymore.

Logical consequences by loving and forgiving parents

High School Mistakes	Long-term Goals: Work Ethic
"I'm 18, rules don't apply." "I'll be in the dorm next year."	Cooperate with authority
Money goes right through their hands.	Defer gratification and develop patience

Note: If you have not yet read the preschool section, I encourage you to do so even if your youngest child is already in high school, because there are many examples that are also helpful with older children. In addition, please remember to refer back to Chapter 4 (Blind Spots), especially the sections labeled "Does this blind spot affect you," and "What to do about it."

MOMENT   Falling in love, thinks it is the "real thing."
LONG-TERM GOAL Emotional calibration: Language of feelings

Now the stakes are high, and we hope the seeds we planted are flourishing. It is very likely that teenagers will imagine their first relationship to be more than it turns out to be, with all the related dangers of poor decision making and broken hearts. Will they share this part of their journey with us? Our ability to guide them will depend on whether they talk to us and whether their ears stay open. If they are not sharing with us, then we have our work cut out for us. We start today, presenting ourselves in a way that helps them see us as their biggest fan (not their biggest critic). If we cannot accomplish this in five days or five weeks, then we work at it for five months or five years. It might help to remember that we do not stop being their parents on the last day of high school and they will not have learned everything that they will ever need to learn by that day. Fifteen- and 16-year-olds are rarely "wise beyond their years." If we can successfully convey to them that we were their age once, that we remember what it was like, that our hearts are in the right place and we hope they let us help them, they just might. (Blind spots: poor listener, naïve)

MOMENT   Copes with stress poorly, either by denial and avoidance, or by getting angry when anxious.
LONG-TERM GOAL Emotional calibration: Thoughts precede feelings

Teenagers who cope with stress well can think things through from several angles. The parent strategies that help at this age include gentle, open-ended questions. "Have you thought about it in this way?" "I wonder if . . ." Honoring sovereignty is never more important than now. Our children need us right in the moment with them, connected to them, seeing them clearly, during the stressful times when they are likely to push us away. One mother told me it helped when she imagined herself to be like the bouncy toy that gets knocked down but pops back up. When her children needed her help but pushed her away, she would retreat a few steps for a while, but always return. And she would return without bitterness or resentment at having been pushed away. She knew many adults who never learned that thoughts precede feelings and she remembered how old she was when she first figured this out. It made perfect sense to her that she would be planting seeds, asking leading questions, and offering suggestions for many years before her children figured this out. (Blind spots: expect payback, insert intent)

MOMENT	Controlled or overly influenced by (or clingy and possessive with) boyfriend or girlfriend.
LONG-TERM GOAL	Interpersonal skills: Boundaries and self-advocacy

It is tricky to know how to help without alienating them by telling them what they should do. Typically the more we listen, the more they talk, and the more they talk to us, the better for them. They are usually more open to statements from us that start with "I" ("I notice . . . ," "I worry about . . .") rather than "you" ("You should break up with her." Or "You shouldn't let him get away with this."). We keep teaching about boundaries. All the times we allowed them to be autonomous and modeled that we knew we did not own them come in handy. They still seem like "our little boy" or "our little girl" but that is not the way they think of themselves and not the way their boyfriend or girlfriend thinks of them. It is not usually helpful for the teenager to simply feel controlled by two powerful people, the friend and the parent. We want to be invited in and perceived as open-minded and interested in learning how to see this new friend through their eyes. Only then are we likely to have influence over their decisions. (Blind spots: poor listener, cloning)

MOMENT	Loud, boisterous, monopolizes conversations, rude, bad manners, shallow or self-centered.
LONG-TERM GOAL	Interpersonal skills: Personal growth process

They can be arrogant and cocky or withdrawn and sullen. They look all grown up and they still act disrespectfully. Continue to discipline with reassurance, resist the urge to mirror them. Breathe in and breathe out. They have their goals that they are still working on, and so do we. We know that we are not always going to handle ourselves the way we want to, because we are human, our plates are full, and we have our own stress to manage. By using our mistakes to model the personal growth process, we can turn a minor negative into a minor positive. They can learn from us how we forgive ourselves and they can see how we forgive them when they are rude or self-centered. We refer back to what we are working on, and in time they will learn to refer back to what they are working on as well. (Blind spots: low tolerance for conflict, lacks confidence)

MOMENT	Steals money from a high school job. Drifting, seems aimless, no sense of direction.
LONG-TERM GOAL	Interpersonal skills: Stress management

Teenagers make bigger mistakes than younger children, but they still need parents. Even (especially) when their mistakes seem huge, we resist judging. We start where they are at, helping them in any way we can. We cannot erase the mess they created, but we can forgive them and at least accompany them on the messy parts of their journey as well. One father told me that whenever his 16-year-old daughter got herself into a particularly unfortunate mess, he always did what he could to prevent her from getting so discouraged and so mad at herself that she might not be able to pick herself up and move forward.

This helped prevent him from "piling on." When the world has already provided the consequences, at least we can protect the connection and provide the reassurance. (Blind spots: overly emotional, expect payback)

MOMENT	Isolates in their room, one-word answers about their day. Not telling us about their plans for the evening. Not open to our guidance (apply for a job early enough, scholarships). Wants to work after high school instead of going to college.
LONG-TERM GOAL	Connected to us: Perceive us accurately as their reservoir of confidence

If they have to go through confusing times, it helps them if they sense that we still believe in them. At the exact same time, if they do not answer our questions about their plans for the evening, they will not have our permission to go out, will not have use of the car, will lose their allowance, or will lose some other privilege that lets them know that we mean business even though we are not yelling and screaming. Our tone is loving and forgiving but our determination to keep them safe and living in accordance with our family rules is evident. If we have to sell a car, or block their use of our cars, we will do so. But we will not throw ourselves in front of a door and try to physically prevent them from leaving or contribute to a deteriorating scene late at night if they come home after curfew. (Blind spots: worships, lacks confidence)

MOMENT	Disagrees with everything we say even before we say it, curfew violations. Decisions made about dating, drinking or drug use during high school. Full of themselves, no time for family, goes out a lot, aloof, indifferent to family. Pursues interest in something parent does not value. When they seem to have no use for us in their lives anymore.
LONG-TERM GOAL	Connected to us: Logical consequences by loving and forgiving parents

Very few teenagers who need professional help show up voluntarily, and there are times when parents have to make calls and schedule meetings. Short of that, we stick with clearly stated rules and expectations, logical consequences and a tone that makes it easy for them to circle back to us as soon as they can. It is more difficult for teenagers to speak disrespectfully to the parents who have been speaking to them respectfully throughout their childhood. If you sense that your mistakes from years ago are being repeated by your teenager, please have confidence that it is reversible. However, the first move will probably have to be yours. If you think you contributed to the interpersonal distance, tell your children what you think happened. This will also be discussed more fully in the next chapter. (Blind spots: low tolerance for conflict, naïve)

MOMENT	"I'm 18, rules don't apply." "I'll be in the dorm next year."
LONG-TERM GOAL	Work ethic: Cooperate with authority

The old refrain about being 18 is not really all that helpful to them. If they would like to move out, they are free to do so, but if they continue to live with us, they follow our rules. We know they will be in the dorm next year, but this year they are still here. While they have more freedoms, they do not have unlimited freedoms. What sometimes is confusing is that our children are starting to look all grown up and we are not necessarily thrilled about the adult they are becoming. If we judge them critically, we might also be indicting our years of parenting, and that can only make things more stressful for everyone. It is better to remember that they will continue to learn and develop new skills and new maturity, and that if they are still close to us we will still be able to help. (Blind spots: expect payback, lacks confidence)

MOMENT	Money goes right through their hands.
LONG-TERM GOAL	Work ethic: Defer gratification and develop patience

Instead of trying to control what they do with their money, we can stop giving them ours. In addition, things they are not used to paying for (cell phone, transportation expenses, and car insurance) can become their responsibility. Teenagers benefit from our calm and casual communication style—even when we are making decisions they do not like. Nobody benefits when we lose it. (Blind spots: overly emotional, low tolerance for conflict)

COMMUNICATION STRATEGIES

Honoring sovereignty:

> ➤ The mistakes are scarier, but we still do not want to make things worse by our reaction. We already have one problem (their mistake); let us not end up with two.
> ➤ Our first thought at the instant of their high school mistake is still, "How may I use this? What can I teach?"
> ➤ Pay close attention to what we can learn about them from their mistakes. What is the long-term goal that still needs work?
> ➤ It is because we love them so much that we resist feeling too upset if they begin to take their lives in a direction that we think is not best.

Protecting the connection:

> ➤ It is only their continuing connection with us that will allow us influence.
> ➤ "Nothing you can do changes the fact that I am crazy about you."
> ➤ "Just because I love you, that doesn't mean I own you."
> ➤ "We will get through this together. Even though this feels big enough to get the best of us, it is nothing compared to my love and commitment to you, exactly the way you are."

Presenting our lives as models:

> ➤ We are their reservoir of confidence, now more than ever. If their transition into adulthood is going to be less smooth than we had hoped, we want to prevent them from feeling discouraged. As long as they keep moving forward, they will ultimately get to a good place.
> ➤ Especially now that they are surrounded by alcohol and

other weekend temptations, we have to attend to our life as a model.

> Teenagers tend to look to us for "permission" to take risks they should not be taking. Many 16- and 17-year-olds have justified their decisions about alcohol and their behavior at parties by referring to something they saw or heard at home.

> Their thought processes are still developing, and they often fail to grasp the difference between what adults can legally do and what teenagers cannot do.

HIGH SCHOOL DISAPPOINTMENTS AND LONG-TERM GOALS

High School Disappointments	Long-term Goals: Resilience
Fired from job, cut from team, misses out on opportunity. ACT/SAT scores, college application process, senses doors closing. Child does not get "enough" play time on a team sport.	Self-esteem is not contingent on a smooth road

High School Disappointments	Long-term Goals: Emotional Calibration
Self-conscious, pessimistic, worried about the future.	Thoughts precede feelings
A boyfriend or girlfriend is mean to them or breaks up with them.	Sizing
Works harder for disappointing grades than friends work for better grades.	Optimism

High School Disappointments	Long-term Goals: Interpersonal Skills
Child is done with piano or basketball.	Boundaries and self-advocacy
Friend is struggling with depression, eating disorder or some other serious concern.	Stress management

MOMENT	Fired from job, cut from team, misses out on opportunity. ACT/SAT scores, college application process, senses doors closing. Child does not get "enough" play time on a team sport.
LONG-TERM GOAL	Resilience: Self-esteem is not contingent on a smooth road

Teenagers experience bigger disappointments than younger children. That is why we taught them to separate their self-esteem from how their day is going when they were younger. If they are heading for a college on this list rather than that list, at least they will not have to be confused about their worth as a person. When they are younger we encourage them to go as far as they possibly can with their academic career but we have to be ready to reassure them that they are not failures if they are not able to go as far as they (or we) had hoped. It helps them to know that there are many roads in life and that they can all lead to successful futures. (Blind spots: rulebooks, cloning)

MOMENT	Self-conscious, pessimistic, worried about the future.
LONG-TERM GOAL	Emotional calibration: Thoughts precede feelings

If they are overly worried and pessimistic, that might mean we have to work with them more on how thoughts influence feelings and how thoughts can be modified. Are they comparing themselves to others or to benchmarks? Do they think there is only one right way to move into adulthood, and they are not doing it? Do they need to be reassured that detours are acceptable and may lead back to the desired road after an extra year or two? If they still need to work on how their thoughts affect how they are feeling, then we continue to work with them on this. (Blind spots: myth of smooth road, poor listener)

MOMENT	Child is done with piano or basketball.
LONG-TERM GOAL	Interpersonal skills: Boundaries and self-advocacy

When they were little, we signed them up for what we thought they might enjoy. Maybe over the years if they complained about a sport or piano lessons, we talked to them about sticking with a commitment and not being a quitter. Maybe we were hoping for a college scholarship. But if they are done, they are done, and it is time for us to support them as they live their life. We already had our turn. Not only do we have to remember that they may not share our passion for a particular sport or musical instrument, but we have to convince them that all we want is for them to find *their interests* and pursue them, not to make them pursue *our interests*. (Blind spots: rulebooks, cloning)

MOMENT	Friend is struggling with depression, eating disorder or some other serious concern.
LONG-TERM GOAL	Interpersonal skills: Stress management

We want them to support those who are hurting—but not get dragged down themselves. Our role is to teach self-preservation while reaching out. So much may depend on whether they view us as approachable. Will they talk to us about what their friend is going through so we can give them advice? Will they fall into a "junior counselor" role and end up overwhelmed by the responsibility of trying to help? The irony is that they may decide whether to share with us based on how we handled their messy room or forgotten school project years ago. (Blind spots: low tolerance for conflict, poor listener)

MOMENT	A boyfriend or girlfriend is mean to them or breaks up with them.
LONG-TERM GOAL	Emotional calibration: Sizing

As predictable as this is to us, they always seem to be surprised! As with other life events, it is not the breakup that has to make them feel any certain way. Our role is to help them maintain their sense of balance and perspective while they work through the stages of grieving. We know it seems big to them right now and we have a lifetime of conversations with them to refer back to. All the times that seemed big that became small after a month or two, now become the references for this. This too shall pass. (Blind spots: overly emotional, cloning)

MOMENT	Works harder for disappointing grades than friends work for better grades.
LONG-TERM GOAL	Emotional calibration: Optimism

If they work hard, they should feel proud of themselves no matter what grade they get. The bigger nightmare is not the lower grade, it is the possibility of discouragement that leads to giving up. Here is the payoff for all the times we refused to judge them according to rulebooks. If a door closes, a window opens. They will find the right path to take for them, and it undoubtedly will have nothing to do with their weakest academic subject in high school. (Blind spots: expect payback, cloning)

COMMUNICATION STRATEGIES

Honoring sovereignty:

> ➤ We continue honoring sovereignty as we have been. What might be different is the sense of urgency that often accompanies the end of childhood.
> ➤ Resist panicking. We focus on the relationship between our teenagers and us, not on their relationship with their world.
> ➤ We want to help them deal with whatever comes their way, including disappointments pertaining to academics, athletics or friendships.
> ➤ It is from us that they get the inner strength to do the best they can with what they have.

Protecting the connection:

> ➤ They experience disappointments, but they are never a disappointment to us.
> ➤ With us by their side, they are more capable of bouncing back from their losses.
> ➤ Remember to enjoy them! You do not have to devote 100 percent of your time with them to pushing and prodding, cajoling and criticizing.
> ➤ They will be "launched" in the blink of an eye. If you do not figure out how to connect during the high school years, you might look back on that with regret.

Presenting our lives as models:

> ➤ Talk about how often adults change careers. Clarify that you really do mean "careers," not just jobs.
> ➤ Whatever they do during the first year after high school is just what they do for that year. If they are not able to go to their dream college now, they can try again next year.
> ➤ Even if you are concerned, convince them that their road is a reasonable one for them, and can always lead them to

new and different roads. You might say, "Some teenagers work for a year after high school and then are more ready (and more successful) when they start college the following year."

› Refer to successful relatives who were "late bloomers." Uncles or aunts who were successful in business or in life may have struggled during their high school years.

TABLE ONE—LONG-TERM GOALS (Reprinted from Chapter 1)

1. Resilience
- ➤ What worth is based on
- ➤ Self-esteem is not contingent on a smooth road
- ➤ Anticipate disappointments

2. Emotional calibration
- ➤ Language of feelings
- ➤ Closure
- ➤ Optimism
- ➤ Thoughts precede feelings
- ➤ Change and loss
- ➤ Sizing

3. Interpersonal skills
- ➤ Boundaries and self-advocacy
- ➤ Communication and conflict-resolution skills
- ➤ Compassion
- ➤ Trust
- ➤ Personal growth process
- ➤ Internal locus of control
- ➤ Stress management

4. Connected to us
- ➤ Perceive us accurately as their reservoir of confidence
- ➤ Logical consequences by loving and forgiving parents

5. Work ethic
- ➤ Defer gratification and develop patience
- ➤ Cooperate with authority
- ➤ Importance of education
- ➤ Ability to work with anyone

Chapter 9

But My Child . . .

Insightful parenting requires looking inward, understanding blind spots, and taking responsibility for what we do. This is always hard work. It is hard work when our children are thriving and cooperating, and it is hard work when they are struggling and challenging.

But our work is still our work, and the goal is still to discipline with reassurance, honor sovereignty, protect the connection and present our lives as role models, regardless of what our children do, or where they are in their development.

The phrase "but my child . . ." was used many times by parents to explain why they responded to their child in a way they later regretted. And since we are all only human, it is inevitable that we will get worn out, and then the worrying, judging, intruding and hesitating blind spots will affect how we view our children. How we parent hinges on our ability to honor our children's sovereignty even when it is most difficult.

As you read these final chapters, imagine a parent in therapy at the point where they are ready to look inward. They might say: "I want to be able to parent in this insightful way, but my child . . . and therefore I am not able to." Here are a few reasons parents have cited to explain their inability to parent insightfully. As with previous examples, it is not meant to be an exhaustive list, rather, just enough of a list to demonstrate how this approach to parenting is about us and for us, regardless of our children's age or life circumstance.

But my child . . .

> Has a serious physical condition (birth trauma, diabetes, cardiac or respiratory weakness, Down Syndrome).
> Has a mental health condition (Asperger's, depression, bipolar, anxiety, obsessive-compulsive disorder, attention deficit).
> Has a learning disability.
> Is adopted.
> Has to deal with a messy divorce.
> Is the oldest (middle, youngest, only) child.
> Is already in high school.

PHYSICAL CONDITIONS

Parents of children with serious physical conditions often become experts at honoring sovereignty. Usually the more serious the physical condition, the more obvious it is that goals and dreams will need to be individualized. If children are struggling with diabetes or asthma, parents "start where their children are at" and help them in every way possible. The children are on their own road, and it is usually possible *to see this clearly.* It is hard to imagine a parent of a child with diabetes getting frustrated with the child because of the extra care needed. And no parent would yell at a child with asthma to "run faster, and don't be a quitter."

The parents of children with physical conditions accompany them on their road, help them accomplish whatever they can accomplish and enjoy all they can enjoy. They become insightful and in tune with the child's needs, and this prevents the worrying, judging, intruding and hesitating blind spots from interfering with parenting. The rest of us can learn a lot about honoring sovereignty from these parents. Once the child's unique circumstances are honored, parents are able to discipline with reassurance and protect the connection.

MENTAL HEALTH CONDITIONS

The visual cues are not always so obvious for mental health conditions. This might be why parents have been known to get angry at children with Attention Deficit Disorder (ADD) for having poor impulse control, or for being annoyed with depressed children for being thin-skinned and easily hurt! In fact, it is common to hear parents of children with ADD recalling times they yelled at their child for acting in a way that is appropriate to their condition. One reason for this might be that without the visual cues, we have a harder time honoring the power of the condition over behavior. For example, we want our children with ADD to talk to us respectfully, be organized and bring home what they need for their homework. When they do not, we have to remember the cause of these behaviors is just as valid as the cause of behavior of the child with diabetes or asthma. When we see this clearly, we honor our children's sovereignty.

It is outside the scope of this book to address in detail the unique challenges of parenting a child with physical or mental health disorders. In fact, there is a great deal of difference within the population of children with any of these or other conditions. What is consistent is how critical it is for parents to honor their children's uniqueness at every moment of their lives.

If you have a child with Asperger's syndrome, you are undoubtedly already an expert on this condition. The parent who comes to mind here is the father who always assumed he would share his love for sports with his only son. This son had many interests but absolutely no interest in playing sports, learning about sports, or watching sports on television. For several years before therapy, this father tried everything he could think of to change his son into the son he always wanted. When he acknowledged the power of Asperger's to deprive him of this dream, he let go of that dream, and was better able to honor his son's sovereignty.

Once children have been assessed and diagnosed, and parents start learning about the condition, the past makes more sense. The years prior to diagnosis may have been a confusing time for all, with no context in which to understand the challenges presented by the child. Parents often describe with sadness their memories of responding to certain behaviors of their child that later turned out to be due to a physical or mental health condition. This refrain has been repeated by parents of children with depression, anxiety and bipolar and obsessive compulsive disorders.

It was not possible for them to honor their child's sovereignty because they were not yet able to see their child's behavior accurately. After diagnosis, parents can explain this to their child as best they can, after considering the child's age. Then they can move on. The future will depend on whether the parent is able to see the mental health condition as clearly as the parents of a child with a physical condition.

This also highlights the advantage of seeking a full assessment even if you are convinced it will only "rule out" a condition. There can be significant benefits to such "rule out" assessments for the simple reason that the same behavior can have different meanings for different children. It makes sense to us that a child in sixth grade with Attention Deficit Disorder would be impulsive and disorganized. To follow the exact same discipline plan as we would for a 6th-grade student without ADD would not be honoring the sovereignty of the student with the condition.

If an assessment is obtained and various conditions are ruled out, it reassures us and permits the use of ordinary parenting strategies. Now, we can confidently set the bar academically and behaviorally and hold them accountable. If the assessment yields a diagnosis but is not convincing, parents can always defer any action, perhaps revisit the issue in a year or two, and seek a second opinion if the problems continue. Parents are always in charge of such important matters. Others should not be pushy, but it is usually wise to at least consider the observations of school personnel, especially teachers in the younger grades, who spend six or seven hours a day with the children.

LEARNING DISABILITY

When there is a learning disability or some other legitimate barrier to academic success, parents have to advocate for their children and encourage them to reach their full potential. But they also need to honor sovereignty by having realistic expectations for what academic success looks like for their child. Young children tend to have parents who believe there are no limits to what they can accomplish, and if it becomes necessary to adjust goals, some effort may be required. Children who struggle with reading, math, spelling or short-term memory already have extra stress in their lives. Our job as parents is not to add more by our reluctance to honor their sovereignty and their limits.

ADOPTION

My children were adopted from South Korea when they were four and seven months old. Perhaps as a result of this, I have worked quite a bit with adopted children in general and interracial adoptions in particular. It is well-known that adopted children sometimes act in inappropriate ways out of an unconscious need to test their parents' commitment to them. It is almost as if they are asking: "Will you still love me if I steal?" "Will you abandon me if I have accidents in the house?" "What will happen if I lie?" "What happens if I lie relentlessly?"

Many books have been written about parenting adopted children. The point here is how this parenting approach pertains to the special needs that are sometimes presented by adoption. If your adopted child tests the connection, how should you proceed? What does honoring sovereignty look like if your child lies or steals for years?

As is clear by now, insightful parenting begins with us looking in the mirror, rather than across the room. If our adopted children test the connection, then our job is to protect the connection. If they test the connection more than other children, it is only because they need additional reassurance that the connection is safe and unaffected by their behavioral mistakes. Their greater need only makes it more urgent for us to do our part well. If the judging blind spots, ("You should not be this way") or the worrying blind spots, ("If they are lying at this age, what will they be like when they are older?"), prevent us from doing our part well, *that is what ultimately influences their future.* If they test the connection and find it safe and protected, they are more likely to improve, with less of a need to test us, as soon as they can.

DIVORCE

You do not have to be a therapist to be familiar with the tendency of divorced parents to blame the other parent for their children's problems in life. While I have no doubt that some ex-spouses make mistakes in their parenting, the trend is still a concerning one. Even when one parent wishes the other would parent differently, there is still the "where to focus" issue. As you recall, we are supposed to focus as much as possible on our relationship with our children and not between our children and their world. Once divorced, the relationship between children and one parent is no longer the domain of the other parent. When there are problems in that relationship, we try to use whatever is happening to teach our children whatever we can. And teaching what we can teach is very different from the following parental rationales: "I would like to be able to parent insightfully, *but my child* has an irresponsible father, and I feel so sad that I just can't bear to follow through with ordinary discipline." Or you might hear: "You bet I intrude. After all he's been through with that mother of his, there is no way I'm going to let him miss out on that field trip just because he forgot to have me sign the permission slip. I'll leave work and get it to him in time for him to get on the bus."

BIRTH ORDER

With all that has been written about birth order, what follows may be unnecessary. However, in therapy when a parent starts talking about birth order, it is more often an obstacle than a help. This might be due to the context. Even though some of what has been written about birth order is probably accurate, the parent referring to birth order is a warning sign of a parent who is not looking inward. Typically, the parent is externalizing and rationalizing why their children are acting a certain way. They might be over-psychologizing (the worrying blind spot) or over-helping (the intruding blind spot). Whether a child is first, middle, last or an only child, they are still responsible for their actions, and we are still responsible for ours.

Chapter 10

But My Children . . . Are Already in High School

With physical and mental health conditions, there is the time before diagnosis and the time after diagnosis. Similarly, birth order, adoption, and divorce are definitive factors that grab our attention and influence our parenting. But what if a parent reads this book, with its emphasis on preparing for adolescence during the years prior to grades six or seven, after their youngest is already in high school?

A parent might read this book before their children are teenagers and find it useful in ordinary times and extraordinary times, with diagnoses or without diagnoses, with adopted children, blended families, etc. But parents of teenagers might read this book and wish they had read it when their children were younger. Perhaps there already is a problem with underachieving. Or maybe there is too much distance in the parent-teen relationship. What if the parent sees parenting mistakes in the past five or ten years that inadvertently contributed to the underachieving or the distance? What follows is the response to these questions: "What if I haven't been parenting this way? Is it too late?"

ACKNOWLEDGING AND REPAIRING DAMAGE

Once your children are in high school, you might be concerned about damage done that cannot be repaired. Try not to worry so much about that. Parents who get lost in past regrets have trouble doing what they can in the present. Think about it this way instead. Fortunately, older children will be able to understand high-level conversations dealing with complicated concepts like regrets about parenting and missed moments.

If you are intrigued and interested in parenting in the way described in this book, that is your new starting point. We cannot do anything about last week, last month or last year. Even if you were not parenting this way before today, today becomes the point of reference. Prepare for a conversation with your children. Start a notebook, make a list. Beginning today, what are your goals? Use the words provided if they are comfortable words for you, discipline with reassurance, honor sovereignty, protect the connection, present your life as a model, and include the blind spots you think were in your way. Anticipate their questions. They may want to know why now, all of sudden, they should trust that you are going to be able to change? Why not ten years ago? What was it that happened to you when you were growing up that prevented you from being this kind of a parent when they were little? Most parents have a pretty good idea what happened. Be honest with your children even if it affects how they think about their grandparents. Their relationship with you is paramount. Here are a few comments parents shared in therapy sessions from conversations with their teenagers at home.

> "I would get so worried about what was happening, and then I would make things worse instead of making things better."
> "I haven't been protecting the space between us."
> "My heart was in the right place, but that doesn't change the fact that I handled myself poorly."
> "I was trying to make sure you got the right grades so you would be able to get into the best college."
> "I thought I was supposed to 'get in your face' whenever you make a mistake."
> "I wish I had done a bunch of things differently."
> "I think you might have thought I was disappointed in you."

> ➤ "I think I made a complete pest of myself for the last few years."
> ➤ "I should have used a different voice for the less serious things so you would have still been hearing my more serious voice for dating, drinking, driving issues."
> ➤ "I wish I had yelled and threatened less, and listened more and followed through more."

Parents in therapy would refer to the therapy as the new point of reference, using a "now that I know this" explanation. Similarly, attending a seminar about parenting, or reading a parenting book, can help start the conversation with teenagers. There is no rewind button in life. We cannot go back in time and know what we did not know. But we can change today and all the tomorrows.

A NEW USE FOR MISTAKES

If you are comfortable with the idea of celebrating children's mistakes and intend to parent by looking for teaching opportunities, share this with your teenager and acknowledge that you will continue to make mistakes as well. The pace of change for parents, as well as for children, is slow, and progress is always uneven. While you are telling them how you wish you handled their mistakes from years ago, set the stage for your uneven progress and your future mistakes. You probably will not be able to change on a dime, commit yourself to change how you parent and never make a mistake. For example, if you have struggled with the judging blind spots, you will probably still compare your teenager to an invisible rulebook, appear as if your love is conditional, expect payback and inaccurately insert intent from time to time.

The change will not be that you never again make mistakes. The change will be in what you do after a mistake. In the past, you may have blamed your child for your response or rationalized your intense or impatient reaction in certain ways. Perhaps by saying "they need to know how much this matters to me." Now when you make a mistake, you can take responsibility for it, apologize and look at your own mistake for its teaching opportunity. Most teenagers will appreciate that their parents are not perfect people and are working on their own personal growth program. This is using our life as a model to show them a healthy way to handle their own mistakes.

It can be helpful, although sometimes uncomfortable, to look back with your teenager and review certain scenes that you now wish you handled differently. Sometimes there are one or two that exemplify dozens of other times, and by facing the one or two, the hurt feelings from the dozens of others can be soothed as well. For example, if you and your child were in a pattern of interaction that included two mistakes: they ignored you and then you yelled, you can revisit it, own your part and say how you wish you had handled your part. The following strategies may be useful:

> The more specific the better. Instead of referring to "whenever you ignored me and I yelled," say, "Remember the time when I was trying to get you to take out the garbage and you wanted to finish watching your show?"
> Explain what you think happened. "I thought you were turning into a slacker, and I was trying to help you use your potential. I was worried that you would never get into college."
> Refer to your blind spots. "I was trying so hard to help you with your problems that I became a complete nuisance. That is when we started to drift."
> What do you wish you knew then? "If only someone told me I was supposed to protect the connection rather than make sure your room was always clean, maybe I would have been able to parent differently all these years." Or "I thought if I didn't get your room clean right that minute, then I wasn't a good parent. I really didn't know that as long as you had a consequence for not cooperating that would be enough."

> ▸ "I think I was too controlling over little things when you were younger and you rebelled against me. Now that things are really scary out there, when I try to give you advice to keep you safe, you're not really listening any more."

HONORING SOVEREIGNTY WITH OLDER TEENAGERS

The stakes are high and the times are scary. There is no way around it. Our babies get their driver's licenses, and we do not always know their friends and may not know their friends' parents. They might be more involved in sports, theater or dance than they are home. Boyfriends or girlfriends are involved. There are parties on weekends. What if all this is compounded by a strained relationship between you and your teenager? How are we to honor their sovereignty when the stakes are so high?

We want to have as much *influence* over their lives as we possibly can, especially now. However the key word in that sentence is influence, not power. The goal is to present ourselves to our older teenagers in a way that allows us to have influence over their lives without needless power struggles. It is better they say "thanks for the help," rather than "you're trying to run my life."

After your conversations with your teenager about the past, you may find new openings in the walls they built. To keep them open typically requires deliberate effort. Remember, the influence parents have over teenagers comes from the connection. They are away from us a lot. We are not with them when they make their most important decisions. And they decide what to share with us. We will probably not even know about their scariest times unless they voluntarily tell us. Here are a few examples of ways to convince your teenager that it is influence you seek, not power, and it is the influence to keep them safe and well, not to control their lives.

> ▸ "I love you and I am concerned, but that doesn't make me right about what I'm concerned about."

> ▶ "I want what's best for you, but what's best for you might not be what I think is best for you."
> ▶ "It's the health and safety issues that concern me the most—driving, dating and weekends, not the classes you take, the sports you're in, or what college you go to."
> ▶ "I am not your puppet master, and you are not the puppet. You are on your way to being an adult, and I would very much like to be close to you, not to run things, but to be part of things."
> ▶ "Even though I don't like your boyfriend, he's not my boyfriend. Grandma wasn't too thrilled about Dad at first either. I hope you feel comfortable talking to me about how the relationship is going so I can try to help in any way possible."

Obviously this is harder work than telling them what to do and then telling them again in a louder voice. The communication requires more finesse, like when you are dealing with difficult people at work, especially difficult people who have power. If your career has involved workshops and training sessions on communication skills and conflict resolution, please bring those skills into your relationship with your older teenagers.

More than ever, we pay attention to the dotted line between our children and ourselves. We are responsible for our part and we try to be in a respectful mode at all times, despite what they do or say. Honoring sovereignty is the work parents have to do with all children, including children with special needs, learning or attention issues, physical or mental health conditions and with older teenagers. We look in the mirror and work to be the best "us" we can be, help them as much as we can, while knowing we cannot guarantee them the smooth road in life we wish we could. What might complicate matters is if there are guilt feelings for the past parenting. Try to skip that. We only have the day in front of us, and it would be very unfortunate if feelings of regret led us to parent in the present in unhelpful ways.

Forgive yourself, model for your children that all mistakes are forgivable, and do what you can to regain the intimate connection between you and your teenager.

Let us think back to the two columns discussed earlier. One column is the part of their lives that we still control, the other column is the part we acknowledge is no longer ours. Try to sound joyous about this. Depending on how well they are managing their life, this can take some effort. Safety and health issues (e.g., curfews, doctor's appointments and medication, rules about alcohol and drug use) are best retained in our column. Teenagers usually allow this to the extent that their column includes what is most important to them (e.g., choice of friends, level of academic achievement, part-time jobs, the college application process). While it is hard to believe when our children are younger, it ultimately is up to them to choose a college. And by all means, do everything possible to prevent conflicts over the smallest matters like hairstyles, or how they dress, which decreases your influence over the largest matters, especially the ones that could take them away from us.

ACADEMICS

If their high school career is not going well, we want to do more than simply add tension by our strategies. No matter how much we assumed they would go directly from high school to an excellent four-year college, if that begins to look unlikely, we should try to prevent them from becoming discouraged. The worst case scenario may not be working for a year after high school or going to a two-year college, it might be giving up and deciding that there is no use to keep trying. As long as they are still connected to us, they can turn their lives around right before the end of high school or right after the end of high school. Honoring sovereignty is sometimes adjusting the plan, even if it impacts hopes and dreams we have for our children's future. And, like everything else discussed in this book, it is hard work. Here are a few thoughts that can help you stay focused on the connection with your teenager and not get too distracted by their academic career.

> ▸ There are many roads to adulthood. Not everyone goes straight to their first choice four-year college. There is no shame in going to a two-year college and then transferring to a four-year college.
> ▸ High school performance does not necessarily predict adult success. In many respects, life is easier than high school. Instead of having to be good in many subjects at the same time, including ones that are not interesting, when they are adults, they will only have to be good at one thing.
> ▸ The college entrance exams (ACT, SAT) may influence their college options, but they should not be perceived by our older teenagers as measures of their worth as a person.
> ▸ It is not which college they go to; it is who they are when they get there.
> ▸ There are 4,400 colleges, but our teenagers only have one family. Let us get the family part right even if the college part is a little disappointing.
> ▸ The goal is not getting into the best college, it is getting into the best college for the child.

DRIVING

Most teenagers get their driver's license when they are 16 (or whenever they can), and it makes sense that they would be excited about this and that we would encourage it. However, there are a few exceptions and a few things to consider.

If you have reasons to be concerned that they might not be a good driver, perhaps because of an attention issue or a reckless attitude in general, we could allow the driver's license but only limited use of the car for the first six or twelve months. That is, they could get their driver's license "on time" but be restricted to daylight hours at first, with limits on who can be in the car with them until we are confident of their safety. I do not recommend unlimited access to a family car at 16, and I do not recommend that teenagers own their own car until at least the age of 18. And then, even if your family can afford to help with the purchase, the car should be purchased primarily with their money or with a loan they are required to repay. If insurance rates are lower with good grades ("B" average), you might offer to pay the "good grades" rate, or half the good grades rate, but they should certainly pay for the increased premium if their grades are lower. This is a good life lesson for them and protects the connection at the same time. Avoid paying the higher premium and nagging them to get their grades up. Also, by keeping control over the family car, you are free to connect access to your car with day-to-day issues like manners, chores and grades.

HOLDING ON AND LETTING GO

The phrase used most often to describe parenting older teenagers is "holding on and letting go" and you can certainly see why. It is most definitely not simply letting go. They still need us, in some ways more than ever. They need us more than they know and more than they wish they did. While we might be tempted to help them with many areas of their lives, it is best to devote our energies to honoring their sovereignty and protecting the connection so we will be able to help them with the critical areas. If the hesitating blind spots interfered when your children were younger, be careful about overcompensating now and trying to crack down on everything all at once.

Parents tend to see the 18th birthday and high school graduation as the end of the road, and it absolutely is not. The mistakes and disappointments do get bigger and scarier, and the children start to look like young adults even while their behavior is screaming "not ready" for adulthood. But have faith that they will continue to mature and develop through the transition to adulthood. We did not have our act completely together on our 18th birthday, and they will not either. They may start off in one college and transfer to another. Most of us did not know what we were going to do with our lives at this age, and those of us who did may have changed careers (not just jobs, but careers) years later. It is better to allow them to be 18 as it really is, rather than as we wish it was. Remember that our parents did not necessarily know what was right for us just because they were our parents. In fact, when we were 18, did we think our parents even knew us as people at all? Now that it is our turn to be the parents of 18-year-olds, we have to resist the feeling that we know best just because we love them.

INCREASING THE SHARING

The older they get, the more it comes down to whether they freely choose to share with us. But what if everything was not perfect during their pre-adolescent years, and now they are reluctant to share? Ideally, the conversations about the past can help clear the air. And the two-column exercise ought to help by clarifying the power they have over most of their life and reducing the tension about the parts we keep in our column.

First, here is a piece of good news. Teenagers love to talk and they love to share. They even love to argue and debate. Anyone who has ever been on a high school retreat, a weekend tournament, or a mission or scouting trip knows that there is no shortage of words being thrown around. So our task, while daunting, is not impossible. We do not have to teach them to share, just to share with us.

There might be areas of interest that they love to talk about, though probably not how the test went today, how their friends are acting or how they are doing on the project due next week. Anything they are willing to talk about becomes our favorite topic of conversation. The more their words happen near our ears the better. Many mothers have feigned interest in sports and many fathers have listened to their teenage daughters talk about minute details of high school relationship drama for the sole purpose of increasing the sharing.

When the goal is to increase the sharing, then the strategy is not to constantly correct them, and not to criticize beliefs they have that we do not share. Remember the autonomy work they are doing, and it will make sense that they have to bait us and shock us from time to time. It is almost always better to hear them out on controversial topics (e.g., they do not believe everyone has to go to college, the death penalty is good or bad, abortion should be allowed or restricted), and generally it will be positions you do not hold. There is very little to gain from tension over such conversations. And there may be much to gain by viewing these conversations as opportunities to reintroduce ourselves as approachable parents who honor their sovereignty and their right to hold positions on topics that differ from ours. In this way, whenever they are done baiting us, and hinting about the person they are becoming, they may actually tell us.

If we know why they hold back from sharing with us we can put that into words. "You probably assume I'll judge you, get angry, tell you where you're messing up. And that makes sense because of where we've been. I hope you try again to share with me so I can show you I've changed." If they are not sharing because they predict you will try to help too much, put that into words as well. "I used to think I was supposed to intrude in every single part of your life, but now I know the difference between listening and caring and taking over." If it is our worrying that turns them off, try giving them permission to end the conversation at any time, without getting into trouble. Maybe you could encourage them to use the timeout sign from sports (two hands together making a "T"). Maybe if they know they can end a conversation, they will be more willing to start one.

More important than any single conversation, we view each for its ability to smooth the way to the next. We want them to share more next week than this week. When they make their high school mistakes (e.g., curfew violations) and need consequences, we try to handle ourselves so that no interpersonal distance is created by our words, our tone of voice or the look in our eyes. If there are recurring problems, see if they will brainstorm with you in between confrontations, when things are calm, about how to handle them better in the future. Even if they storm off or think it is unnecessary or unlikely to help, they may notice and appreciate that you tried. And as in years past, there may be no better time to convince them that we have changed than at the times of their mistakes. The following list contains ideas on how you can express yourself to your high school student so they are less likely to get defensive, and more likely to circle back to you.

> "Neither of us was at our best last night when you came home after curfew. Any ideas on what we could do differently next time?"
> "You know the drill. When you miss curfew, you can't use the car for a week. But mainly I'd like to talk about how concerned I was."
> "I love you. I worry."
> "This is what I notice. How may I help?"
> "The more I know the less anxious I am."
> "When you're not home on time, my imagination gets the best of me."
> "You'll have more freedoms as my trust and confidence in you grows."

SHARING AS WELL AS ASKING QUESTIONS

It is too easy to fall into a pattern of non-stop questioning. The older teenagers are gone a lot. We need to know where they are going, who they are going to be with, and we want to know so much more. If we are not careful, we might be perceived by them as constant interrogators. One obvious solution is to attend to what comes out of our mouth and make sure there is a balance between questions asked, and other, friendlier conversations. Parenting is a relationship between two people. We should be able to hold up our end of the conversation and bring to the relationship interesting topics to discuss. After all, we do this in all of our other relationships! What are you interested in, besides making sure they are safe and thriving? Current events? The environment? Your volunteer commitments? You might also find they are much more open to talking about other people's problems. You might have a coworker who has a niece who got married at a young age. Chances are good that such an opening would lead to a great conversation, especially if there is no pressure on them to agree with your positions every step of the way. What do they think she should do? What kind of advice would they give her? Then when the conversation is nearing an end, you can always state your values clearly. Even if that ends the conversation, it was about to end anyway! We ought to be able to talk with them about things other than their status. After all, parent-teen conversations are not all supposed to resemble an annual review with a supervisor at work.

It is similar to Susan's experience with her younger children. She knew they needed time with her that was devoted to "anything but tasks." Our older teenagers need conversations with us that are not all interrogations, rule enforcement, and criticisms. Since we know some of the conversations are going to have to be that way it becomes important to go out of our way to share topics they might enjoy and to listen to whatever they are willing to share. It would be great if 25 percent of the conversations with our high school juniors and seniors were about tasks and supervision and 75 percent were about connecting and sharing.

WEEKENDS

I saved weekends for the end of the book. Weekends are when the risks are usually taken. At the risk of sounding too dramatic, all of our parenting culminates around weekends, driving, overnights, drinking, drugs, dating and sexual activity. One hundred percent of parents (or more!) of older high school students look back at what they used to think was serious and are astounded. In retrospect, with the wisdom of hindsight, it is clear that only their connection with us can keep them safe when they are away from us, with their friends, in the car, at parties, or in someone else's arms.

Many parents start therapy because of concerns in these areas, and their experiences helped develop the preventative approach described in this book. This last section highlights the strategies most likely to keep teenagers safe on weekends. First is a "Best Practices" document developed in partnership with a parent association at a local high school.

BEST PRACTICES

> - Set the consequence for first use of alcohol or marijuana very high.
> - Make sure they know what you have decided the consequence will be.
> - Welcome their friends in your home as long as there has been a chance for parents to talk.
> - Introduce yourself to parents when you drop your child off at someone's house.
> - Call the other parent, and welcome calls from other parents.
> - Always call before and occasionally call after to compare notes.
> - Friends are not to bring any of their own beverages into your home.
> - Tell your teenager to leave any gathering where there is any drinking or drugs.
> - Call parents if it turns out there was alcohol or marijuana use in your home.
> - Be visible at the party. Walk through, fill the chip bowl, etc.
> - Set the time when you would like the party to end, and stay up until everyone is gone.
> - Wait up for them, kiss them goodnight.

> It is over when it is over. No after-event events.
> Do not say "yes" to any kind of hotel party or spring break trips without adults.
> Be reluctant to say "yes" to last minute requests for sleepovers.
> Remember: Teenagers notice what their parents do and what their friends' parents do.

The importance of keeping our teenagers safe on weekends by protecting their connection with us has never been clearer. Here are a few additional parent beliefs and strategies that seem to affect the decisions teenagers make about weekends.

> Twenty-one is considered an appropriate minimum age for drinking, and this is talked about frequently throughout childhood. We do not pick which laws to obey and which laws not to obey.
> There is no expectation that high school kids will experiment with beer or wine, no belief that teenagers need to practice drinking for college.
> Do not give the allusion that drinking is acceptable as long as the drinking is done at home.
> Alcohol is not automatically a part of every social event the parents have.
> Parents' guests are not welcomed at the door and asked what they are drinking at the same instant, as if the party starts with the first drink.
> At their loosest moment, parents remember that their children are watching and may select that moment to decide to be like them.
> Teenagers do not typically grasp the difference between what is reasonable behavior for a 40-year-old and what is still illegal and ill-advised for a 16-year-old.

CONCERNS ABOUT A FRIEND

If you have a terrific connection with your teenagers, they may tell you about their friends and what their friends are doing with their weekends. For the most part, this is a good thing, but if something is shared unexpectedly, you may be unsure what to do with the information. Is it part of your relationship with your teenager and confidential? Is it the type of problem with such frightening possible outcomes that you feel compelled to contact the friend's parents? It is best to have things clear in advance.

One strategy is to encourage your teenager to feel free to share about their friends without mentioning names. This way they can share fully and you can give them advice without being in a position to call the friend's parents. This immediately helps your child by allowing them to get ideas and support from you. In addition, teenagers will frequently decide, after a conversation or two with us, that they actually would like us to make the phone call and then empower us to do so by (deliberately) choosing to tell us the name of their friend. Another point worth making ahead of time is that there might be times when you have to call someone. For example, if one of their friends was talking about suicide, it is almost always best to call the parents, even if you have never met them or talked with them by telephone.

BEGINNING OF THEIR JOURNEY

The summer after high school is either the end of their childhood or the beginning of their journey, depending on how we choose to view it. Their world lies ahead of them with many opportunities. If we are not careful, we might focus too much on what we, or they, could have done differently or on how things would have looked at this time "if only." That is a good trap to avoid.

As always, try to keep your focus on the space between you and your teenager, rather than between your teenager and their new adventure. They have so much to think about, and so much to sort through. Their friends will be scattering to their own futures, and the security of the familiar is about to be replaced with the insecurity of the unknown. Expect a roller coaster summer.

Your "little boy" or "little girl" is a high school graduate. They may have to convince you, and themselves, that they will not miss you in September. And they may try to accomplish this by being completely obnoxious and self-absorbed for the next three months! They may act as if they deserve the Nobel Prize for graduating high school, as if no one has ever accomplished such a thing before.

Try to remember that they have a lot to deal with emotionally, even if all they seem to do is hop from one graduation party to another, with endless laughter and endless tears, and a summer of good-byes. But they only have 18-year-old skills and 18-year-old emotions to see them through this time. Instead of judging them, worrying and intruding, let go of their list of things to do, and hang on to the connection. In the end, it is really all we have.

And that brings us to the end of this book, as well. The last point I want to make is about how much this book is asking you to do.

It is easier for me to convey to a parent in my office, rather than through the written word, that I know how hard it is to do this work. Please know that it is hard for everyone. The four general principles (disciplining with reassurance, honoring sovereignty, protecting the connection and presenting our lives as models) sound like fluff, until you try to parent according to them every moment of every day, no matter what your children are doing. Very few of us were parented in this kind and gentle way.

You may ask, and I have wondered, how realistic is it to ask you to develop new viewing skills so you will be able to use every mistake and disappointment in a way that moves your children towards their long-term goals? The families where I live are just as "crazy busy" as your family is. Many parents have told me in exactly these words that, "it is all we can do just to get through the day."

While our goal is to parent insightfully every minute of every day, very few of us can achieve that goal. However, I believe that *we can set our goals that high, build in self-forgiveness, and parent according to these principles as often as we can.* Baseball players do not get a hit every time at bat, and we probably do not have to go ten for ten either. And we can use the times when we are worn out, and act in a way that we later regret, to teach about forgiveness and humility. Our children will need to know how to forgive themselves for mistakes they make, and we can show them through our model how it is done.

The principles require hard work, keeping the long-term goals in focus is hard work, and understanding our blind spots is hard work. Judging feels like parenting to a parent with that blind spot. And it is the same with the worrying, intruding and hesitating blind spots. Developing insight into our blind spots can be freeing. It helps us connect with our children in a way that allows us to see them for who they are and to see what they need to learn. When we parent with that kind of insight, we will be able to make the moments count.

Mistakes

PRESCHOOL MISTAKES

> Morning routine, getting out of the house on time.
> Behavior problems in public, meltdowns, tantrums.
> Difficulties with siblings, teasing, fighting.
> Food in their room, they say it is not theirs.
> Selfish, self-centered, trouble sharing, snotty, whiny.
> Do not play well with friend on a play date, do not take turns, trouble sharing.
> Inappropriate behavior at mealtimes, not coming when called, not staying seated, making silly noises, finicky eater.
> Hit (or bit) a peer in day care.
> Trouble falling asleep, vague physical complaints.
> Sibling gets all the attention because of a birthday or sports event. Have to wait, e.g., delayed at airport, get frustrated easily.
> Do not want to try new things, accidents, bedwetting.
> Say "I hate you," or "You're the meanest mom in the whole world" to the parent.
> Getting to bed on time, brushing their teeth, or bath time.
> Putting toys away, making their bed, keeping their room clean.
> Throw tantrums in stores.

KINDERGARTEN–SECOND GRADE MISTAKES

- ➤ Sibling rivalry, bickering in the car.
- ➤ Do not play well with a friend, mean to pets, say unkind things.
- ➤ Lying, manipulate one parent against the other, say the teacher lied.
- ➤ Whiny, demanding, rude, talk back, moody, irritable, bossy, obnoxious, torment younger siblings, complaining, moping. Bossy with friends, take things from other kids at school.
- ➤ Crying jags. Demand parent's undivided attention.
- ➤ Say: "No, you can't make me."
- ➤ Refuse to eat during mealtimes and then complain of being hungry between meals.
- ➤ Dawdle in the morning.
- ➤ Lose glasses or other expensive things.
- ➤ Act like a spoiled child: "I want this, I want that."
- ➤ Difficult mornings, hard to separate.
- ➤ Chores, responsibilities, tidiness, procrastination, task completion.
- ➤ Missing assignments, say they will do something but then do not.
- ➤ Do not put their toys away, bed does not get made.
- ➤ Are afraid to try new things.
- ➤ Refuse to go to school, say "I hate school", call from nurse's office.
- ➤ Last minute refusal to go to a birthday party they had been looking forward to.
- ➤ Tattling, cry baby.

THIRD–FIFTH GRADE MISTAKES

- ➤ Say they did not do it (when they did).
- ➤ Steal something, hide food, eat junk, lie about it. Push, shove, inappropriate use of hands.

- Behavior problems at family gathering.
- Take something that does not belong to them, lose/break something.
- Temper/angry outbursts, deal with anger poorly, meltdowns. Raise voice, lose temper, slam door. Say: "not fair," or complain about favoritism.
- Show no remorse.
- Say a word that is an inappropriate term for a racial or religious group.
- Watch a "bad" show at a friend's house, cheat on a test, swear on the bus.
- Inappropriate humor (bathroom jokes).
- Complain about being bored, do not play well alone.
- Get frustrated and hit someone.
- Annoyed with us and complain what horrible parents we are.
- Passive-aggressive responses: "I'll do it in a minute. You never told me. I'd do it if you would stop nagging me."
- Refuse to accept responsibility, blame others.
- Impulsive, act without thinking.
- Slam doors, complain about our nagging but do nothing without reminders.
- Talk back, rude to us, roll their eyes, disrespectful to parents, ignore us.
- Repeat the same unacceptable behavior for months.
- Say something is done so they can do something, lie to cover up something.
- Homework takes too long, get down on themselves easily.
- Call from teacher about incomplete assignments or behavior in class.
- Report cards are mixed: comments include "could do better." Sunday night homework surprise (wasted time all weekend, then remembered big project due tomorrow).
- Intense thinker, worried about many things.

> Often anxious, ask same question repeatedly, need a lot of reassurance.
> Overly competitive, poor loser or gloating winner.

SIXTH–EIGHTH GRADE MISTAKES

> Inappropriate use of media, television, movies, computer games, internet, music.
> Follow the lead of a friend (wrong crowd).
> Less than ideal friends, pick a wrong friend.
> Speak inappropriately about the other gender's developing bodies.
> "I forgot, you never told me, in a minute, I said I'll do it, you always nag me."
> Experiment with different styles of dress.
> Rude, seem disrespectful.
> Power struggles and defiance. Argue about small matters (chores) and large matters (attending worship service with the family).
> Unappreciative of parents and fortunate circumstances.
> See us as dumber than dirt, roll their eyes at us, sarcasm. Hard to wake up in the morning, hard to get to bed at night.
> Underachieve, poor attitude towards school.
> Organization problems. Left item needed for school project at home.
> Time management, promptness, plan ahead, not using potential, poor grades.
> Say they do not have any homework in order to be able to do something. Not planning for the project that is due in two weeks.
> Chores are done carelessly. They try to manipulate us. Resist participation in family activities. Boys and pornography. Sneak out of the house.

> Parent overhears an inappropriate conversation between peers in sixth and seventh grades, where they say something discriminatory or disrespectful.
> Do not open up, keep feelings in.
> Too hard on self, everything is a big deal, perfectionistic.
> Complain frequently, but not ready to take action.

HIGH SCHOOL MISTAKES

> Waste time, play video games, talk excessively on the phone.
> Underachieve, poor attitude and effort, do not apply themselves on projects.
> Money goes right through their hands.
> Cope with stress poorly, either by denial and avoidance. Put head in the sand or get angry when anxious.
> Preoccupied with appearance issues (pimple before big dance is a crisis).
> Sound boastful about their accomplishments, shallow or self-centered.
> Talk to parents the way they talk to peers (rude, bad manners).
> Loud, boisterous, monopolizes conversations.
> Isolate in their room, give one word answers about their day, how their life is going. Refuse to conveying information to us about their plans for the evening.
> Not open to our guidance (apply for a job early enough, scholarships).
> Want to work for a year after high school, against parent's wishes.
> Disagree with everything we say even before we say it, curfew violations.
> Decisions made about dating, drinking or drug use during high school.

- ▸ Full of themselves, no time for family, gone a lot, aloof, indifferent to family.
- ▸ Pursue interest in something parent does not value.
- ▸ Stole money from a high school job. Drift, aimless, no sense of direction.
- ▸ Controlled or overly influenced by friends, clingy or possessive with boyfriend or girlfriend, says they are "in love" with first relationship.
- ▸ Choose friends who are bad influences, dating problems.
- ▸ "My boyfriend or girlfriend understands me more than you do."
- ▸ Signs of beer, wine or marijuana use. A close friend is in treatment for alcohol or chemical abuse issues).
- ▸ Do not want us to know their friends' parents.
- ▸ Fall in love, think it is the "real thing."
- ▸ College planning, scholarships, miss important deadlines.
- ▸ Unrealistic re: transition to college
- ▸ "I'm 18, rules don't apply." "I'll be the dorm next year."
- ▸ When they seem to have no use for us in their lives anymore.

Disappointments

PRESCHOOL DISAPPOINTMENTS

- Cry when they lose or miss out on something, crushed by smallest disappointment.
- Play date gets canceled, sibling gets sick and you cannot drive them to the park.
- Transitions, do not want something to end.
- Hard to start something new, accidents, bed-wetting.
- Lose a special object, a new toy breaks.
- Parent goes on business trip and they are sobbing and having trouble sleeping.
- Pet runs away or dies, news events, any scares.
- Separation anxiety, cry at daycare or with babysitter.
- A peer takes something that belongs to them, gets in front of them on line.
- Talk about joining grandpa in heaven.
- World events, something they see or hear on the local news.

KINDERGARTEN–SECOND GRADE DISAPPOINTMENTS

- Overheard an argument between parents.
- Do not feel comfortable in bed at night, want to be with parent.

> Problems sharing and taking turns.
> Trouble making or keeping friends.
> Grandparent (or friend's parent) is ill or dies. Friend's parents get divorced.
> Separation problems, get upset when it is time to leave a friend's house. Bedtime worries.
> Negative thinking. "Nobody likes me. I'm no good in anything."
> Friend moves away. A friend's parent dies at a young age.
> Birthday party invitation does not come.
> Do not seem interested in play dates.
> Have a teacher who is more business-like than overly nurturing.

THIRD—FIFTH GRADE DISAPPOINTMENTS

> Cannot do something they were hoping to do.
> Challenges with friendships, change in status in the peer hierarchy.
> Disciplined by teacher in front of peers.
> Experience discrimination.
> Plan for the day changes and they cannot do something they were hoping to do.
> Seem afraid to do overnights.
> Friend stops being their friend, do not make the talent show.
> Play poorly, team loses because of something they did.
> Excluded, no one to play with at recess, being teased.
> Do not make the team or the talent show.
> Early examples of peer pressure and wanting to be accepted.
> Friend has an untraditional family structure that is confusing for your children.

SIXTH–EIGHTH GRADE DISAPPOINTMENTS

> - Not making a team, do not play much, need extra help in reading or math.
> - Disciplined by teacher or recess supervisor.
> - Not being gifted and talented, bumping into limits (academics or sports).
> - Rumors spread that are hurtful and confusing about your children.
> - Accused unfairly.
> - Enjoy a sport but are not one of the stronger players on the team.
> - Emotional roller coaster.
> - Compare themselves to others and feel bad.
> - Dropped the ball, team lost, teammates angry.
> - Friend stops being their friend, says or sends unkind comments. Come home from school sobbing.
> - Conflict with teacher or coach.
> - Expelled from a group of friends. Girls talking about your children behind their backs.

HIGH SCHOOL DISAPPOINTMENTS

> - Difficulty adjusting to a new school, cut from team.
> - Done with piano or basketball.
> - Work harder for disappointing grades than friends work for better grades.
> - Fired from job, cut from team, miss out on opportunities.
> - College application process is difficult, sense doors closing, college plan changes.
> - Do not get "enough" play time on a team sport.
> - Do not test well, ACT/SAT scores are lower than anticipated.
> - Self-conscious, pessimistic, worried about the future.

> ➤ Boyfriend or girlfriend is mean to them or breaks up with them.
> ➤ When they are hurting over a relationship you think is unhealthy for them.
> ➤ Friend is struggling with depression, eating disorder or some other serious concern.